Then Slowly Came The Aging Soldiers

Then Slowly Came the Aged Soldiers

Second Edition by Curt Sanders

— from a contributed poem written by May Grant Riggs, for Sergeant John W. Elwood's book, *Elwood's Stories of the Old Ringgold Cavalry 1847-1865,* page 317.

Table of Contents:

Colophon

Then Slowly Came The Aged Soldiers

SECOND EDITION.

© 2023 Curt Sanders, all rights reserved. Rights are enforced.

Citation: Curt Sanders, Harrisburg, Pennsylvania: self-published, September 2023.

Curt Sanders
4707 Hillside Road
Harrisburg, Pennsylvania 17109-5203

First Edition: copyright 2020.

Printed by lulu.com — a B Corporation.

Cover Photograph: "Pension Tree Group — Pennsylvania Soldiers and Sailors Home, Erie, PA." — circa 1897, partial image, Library of Congress Prints and Photographs Division Washington, D.C.

ISBN: 978-1-7324538-4-5
1. Genealogy.
2. American History.

Made in the United States of America.

Acknowledgments

"No man is an island entire of itself; every man is a piece of the continent, a part of the main..." — John Donne

...and so are acknowledgments and dedications! I pieced this tome together from many origins to whom I am indebted. To wit:

Chapter 2: Sgt. Davis's Lucky Day

- **Larry E. Hoover**, Elizabethtown, Pennsylvania, cousin, for his devoted work and preservation of the Davis family and history.
- The late **Karen Sue Eberly** (1951-2019) for photographic preservation and our mutual cousin **Beth Ann Thomas Powers,** who became her custodian.

Chapter 3: The Horsemen of Michigan

- **Elisabeth Clare Martin Johnson**, Washington, cousin, for her diligent and devoted research on the Kilbourne and Aldrich families.
- **Vicki Cox**, Michigan, cousin, for her early assistance to the Kilbourne and Aldrich families.
- The late **Hiram Clark Martin** (1937-1982), Kalamazoo, Michigan, cousin, for his assistance on the Kilbourne family. His letters are still fondly remembered by me.
- The late **Vena Emily Kilbourne Doyle** (1898-1995), great-aunt, for her patience with me in prying out her wealth of knowledge while plying me with her chocolate chip cookies. Thank you for bequeathing the family photographs to me.

Chapter 4: Neighbors and Kin

- The late **Nannie Virginia Shulley** (1904-1998), cousin, for keeping records and patience when pestered for information during innumerable interviews. Although only seven years old when he died, she personally knew Grandpa Shulley and "his stories" and became the caretaker of his memorabilia. Thank you for bequeathing me some indispensable photographs and history.
- The late **Blanche Ellen Shulley Freeman,** cousin (1914-2014), for her assistance.
- The late **Maysie Naomi Sanders Riley** (1924-2012), cousin, for her perseverance and devotion to family history. I have fond memories resolving our research at her kitchen table. Thank you, May.
- **John Lunceford**, Indiana.

Chapter 5: Those Magnificent Horsemen

- The late **Albert Louis Rose** (1923-2020), cousin, a World War II hero who I owe much to his generosity, and skilled expertise in research. His thirty-year collaboration can never be replaced.
- Again, to the late **Maysie Naomi Sanders Riley** (see chapter 4).
- **Brian Lee Cullison**, cousin, along with his late mother, **Dona Jean Sanders Cullison** of Illinois, for his care of the family, particularly photographs, and the western branches of the Sanders family.
- **Debra Lucille Bailey Trail** of Washington, cousin, for her committed dedication and professionalism to the family story and research.

Chapter 6: The Substitute

- The late **Dudley Howard Dohner,** cousin (1930-1997), for his copious Dohner newsletters, family reunions and dedication to the family.
- The late **William Paul Doner**, cousin (1903-1992), for his contribution to family history, insight and love of classical music. Johan Sibelius welcomed you to the Pearly Gates.

To All:

- To my friend, **Janelle Simmons**, for her encouragement and critical eye, first edit, and criticism when I needed it.
- To my friend, **Gerald L. Waln**, for his entreat to keep on writing about family history.
- And, of course, to my **family** at large for their support and contributing family Bibles, stories and moral support over the years. I could not have done it without them!
- To the many local newspapers and the often nosy journalists and wannabe stringers who wanted to get a story but gave a history. Those one-liner gossipy iotas were often revealing essential marginalia in history. The social media of the day, these unsung heroes get a heavy dose of praise. Let us hope the twenty-first century an onward honors the craft in the era of *sans* paper.
- Acknowledging the online Internet sources, www.familysearch.org, www.ancestry.com, MyHeritage.com and, www.newspapers.com, and many others, for digitalizing records and presenting them to the world. No more groping through files in library stacks, dusty courthouses, tramping cemeteries, hours spent slogging through microfilm roll after roll looking for that one elusive soul, *et al.* But, heck, it was still fun! Many libraries now continue the tradition with "online" records.
- To our Revolutionary forefathers who had the insight to Constitutionally order a decennial Census since 1790. The Census records have become the meat-and-potatoes of family research and an economic and social snap-shot of our nation.

I am sure I am missing someone from over the past 50 years, so please forgive me for any omission. I may have forgotten you, but history has not.

Preface

Second Edition

It started as an investigation into the pension records of American Civil War veterans in the post-antebellum era, or the "Gilded Age," as Mark Twain pegged it in the United States. I wanted to learn more about ancestral Civil War fathers, what surrounded them, what their service and life were like, and what motivated them to leave family and everything for a small amount of money, some patriotism, and adventure. Initially, I included many different veterans but decided to stick to my great-great-grandfathers and their families.

I was born in south-central Pennsylvania in 1953, only 30 miles from Gettysburg, and 90 years after the battle that hurled that town into history, I ate and slept a constant diet of history, leading to a curiosity that never could be satisfied. My youthful vacations with family to central Michigan and their tales of the family also fed my interest.

What you are about to read is non-fiction, true stories, massaged out of the military and pension records of the subjects, local newspapers, and other sources of information. These essays are *not a definitive genealogy* or Civil War history.

This second edition is an update in some content and book formatting.

The stories you are about to read are mined directly from the pension records of the veterans and their relatives and many primary and secondary sources and stories handed down digitally or orally. It accounts for a postbellum celebration of life, poverty, and the struggle of an army of pensioners.

I dislike abbreviations, so little will be found, excluding those within quotes.

Curt Sanders, September 2023

THROWING LIGHT ON THE SUBJECT

I. An Army of Pensioners

"WHAT THE NATION OWES TO ITS VETERAN DEFENDERS NO SKILL CAN COMPUTE, NO LARGESS CAN REPAY."[1]

As a reward for service and to gain loyalty, Julius Caesar's Roman Army began pensions for it's retiring soldiers in the late first century A.D. "Pensions" for service and/or disabilities carried on through the centuries with diverse inventions and incarnations in various nations and governments thereafter.

Moving forward a few centuries to a new nation called The United States of America, a resolution of the Continental Congress, 26 August 1776, provided commissioned, non-commissioned officers and private soldiers who lost a limb or became disabled in its service, to receive a compensation. As the Revolution progressed, and with flagging loyalties in the Revolutionary Army, it became more urgent to retain the farmer-soldier, disabled by time or injury needing some kind of reimbursement for labor loss.

---

[1] Barrows, Isabel C., editor. National Conference of Charities and Correction, 24th Session, 1897.

By 1782 there was an increase in pay but Congress was unable to fork out the means because of War expenses and it fell upon the states.[2]

The "Pension Office," usually under the Secretary of Interior, (and much later the Department of Veteran Affairs) continued into the post-Revolutionary War and was codified law by 1806.[3]

Pensions were subsequently granted to veterans of the War of 1812, and the Mexican War, 1846-1848.

By July 1862,[4] pension rates increased with new eligibility criteria for all military services since 1861. This "[g]eneral Law prescribed that pension benefits were to be awarded to veterans with War-related disabilities and established a medical screening system for rating and compensating disabilities."[5] As the gruesome War Between the States progressed with alarming casualties, and bulging requests, Congress increased rates and eligibility in July 1864[6] and also by March 1873[7] which included widows and children. The rates and qualifications were complex and differed by military branch and their own definitions and medical examination requirements. It was a byzantine bureaucracy that only desperate veterans charged into the intimating exercise of application.

"There was not just one pension system put in place after the War. Union soldiers were covered under the federal system while each former Confederate state had to create and fund its own pension system. And in a change from previous conflicts, it was not only white male veterans who were covered. African American veterans on the Union side were eligible for pensions from the very beginning. Women were also included both as widows and as veterans (primarily nurses) as time went on. Orphaned children were also eligible for assistance although the process was daunting. Each category had its own set of eligibility rules and benefit limits that changed dramatical-

---

[2] Waite, Edward F. "Veteran's Pensions: The Law and Its Administration From the Revolutionary War to the Civil War," *Harper's* (Volume 86, Issue 512, January, 1893). Text from: Library of Congress American Memory Collection, socialwelfare.library.vcu.edu/social-security/veterans-pensions-early-history/

[3] April 1806, 2 Statute 376.

[4] 12 Statute 566.

[5] Blanck, Peter. "Civil War Pensions and Disability," *Ohio State Law Journal,* Volume 62:109.

[6] 13 Statute 387.

[7] 17 Statute 566.

ly over time and affected politics on both sides of the Mason-Dixon Line."[8]

The economic Panic of 1873 — also known as "The Great Depression" until the name was replaced by the 1930s economic depression, or "The Long Depression, 1873-1879 (1896)"[9] — crushed many of the already sick and disabled veterans of the Civil War. These still healthy vets were not yet elderly, entering into their thirties, but the depression hit them hard and many disabled also applied for relief.

By 1885, now in their forties, the pensioners numbered 324,968 including widows.[10]

"Under the Act of June 27, 1890, [Invalid Pension], it is sufficient that a parent shall be in dependent circumstances at the time of applying for pension, without regard to his condition when the son died; but pension under this act begins at the date of filing the application, instead of from the soldiers death, as in cases established under former laws."[11]

PENSIONS

Procured for Soldiers and Sailors

Disabled in the service of the U. S. Also for heirs of deceased soldiers. Pensions date back to date of discharge or death of soldier. Pensions increased. Address (inclosing stamp) H. S. BERLIN & CO., Attorneys, 610 Ninth St., N.W., Washington, D. C. Lock-Box 592.

---

[8] Gorman, Kathleen L. "Civil War Pensions." *Essential Civil War Curriculum, Virginia Center for Civil War Studies at Virginia Tech.* May 2012. www.essentialcivilwarcurriculum.com/civil-War-pensions.html

[9] Some economic historians extend the depression to 1896. The late 19th century was a boom and bust period of a second industrial revolution and unbridled corruption.

[10] Prechtel-Kluskens, Claire. "A Reasonable Degree of Promptitude, Civil War Pension Application Processing, 1861-1885." *Prologue* (Spring 2010, Volume 42, Number 1).

[11] Waite.

I. An Army of Pensioners

In 1890, The Dependent Pension Act expanded eligibility to veterans disabled *regardless of service during the War.* The pensions became important relief for the cash-strapped men and families of the Great Rebellion. "The men and women who received it needed every dollar of it for their immediate wants. They did not hoard it, but put it at once into circulation. Every sort of business got some benefit. The dry-goods merchants, shoe dealers, grocers, butchers, doctors, real estate owners — everybody, in short, who supply the wants of life — all got a share of the money."[12] Politicians in the U.S.A. were also aware of the financial social security nets in Europe to stave off "the anarchist" unrest which had reached the shores of America.

Already in the financial doldrums from "The Long Depression," the "Panic of 1893" increased the hardships of the now long-in-tooth veterans aging in their fifties. The Panic pushed more veterans into the pension ranks. "The unemployment rate hit 25% in Pennsylvania, 35% in New York, and 43% in Michigan."[13] In Ohio it was estimated to be 50%[14] — states that supplied the majority of Union soldiers and sailors during the War. It became obvious to the politicians that relief for a large body of unemployable voting veterans also became a political expediency.

By December 1893 the Civil War pensioners alone were counted 475,645 — including survivors, widows and children.[15] Other sources claims the ranks swelled to one million pensioners, consuming 42% of the federal income budget. President Theodore Roosevelt went further and enlarged the scope of the 1890 law into an age and service pension by Executive Order November 78, Order number 78, in 1904.[16]

The last major change that affected the post-Civil War veterans came in 1907 *when old age itself was considered a disability.*[17] The law provided a pension for veterans over the age of 62, and widows and children also reaped the benefits. From 1908 to 1920, Congress gave increases based upon age and longevity in military service.

---

[12] "Pensions save the country," *The National Tribune*, Washington, District of Columbia; 20 November 1890, page 8.

[13] "Panic of 1893," en.wikipedia.org/wiki/Panic_of_1893; estimate.

[14] "Panic of 1893," Ohio History Connection. www.ohiohistorycentral.org/w/Panic_of_1893

[15] *Gettysburg Complier,* Gettysburg, Adams County, Pennsylvania, 12 December 1893, page 4 referring to President Grover Cleveland's State-of-the-Union address.

[16] Blanck.

[17] Gorman.

Irene Triplett was the last Civil War Pensioner. Irene is the daughter of veteran Moses Triplett whose second marriage to Elida Hall, 50 years his junior, begot Irene. She collected $73.13 per month[18] before passing away 31 May 2020.

NOTES.

The act of June 27, 1890, requires, in widow's case:

(1) That the soldier served at least *ninety days* in the war of the rebellion and was *honorably discharged*.

(2) Proof of soldier's death (death cause need not have been due to Army service).

(3) That widow is "without other means of support than her daily labor."

(4) That widow was married to soldier prior to June 27, 1890, date of the act.

(5) That all pensions under this act commence from date of receipt of application in the Pension Bureau.

---

[18] Mills, Curt. "U.S. Still Paying a Civil War Pension," *U.S. News & World Report*. 8 August 2016, www.usnews.com/news/articles/2016-08-08/civil-War-vets-pension-still-remains-on-governments-payroll-151-years-after-last-shot-fired

Sgt. William Henry Davis, Jr.
Photograph courtesy of Larry Hoover

II. Sgt. Davis's Lucky Day

"I think we paid dearly for our trip into Pennsylvania… we gave 20 thousand mens lives for a few cattle horses & wagons. I think our confederacy is gone up the spout."[19]

---

[19] Robinson, George Franklin, *Letter*. Company A, 7th South Carolina Infantry Regiment, Kershaw's Brigade, 18 July 1863.

Confederate General Robert E. Lee knew the war was not sustainable; he knew, in the beginning, his army would be primarily defensive — lacking in troops and supplies and hindered by a large geography. Initial victories were a testament to his military skill and experience, but by 1863 he knew skills and the fighting spirit of his men, would not be adequate for a long war. He was cheered for his decisive victory at Chancellorsville in that May, considered his most victorious, but it didn't bring him joy. High casualties, the loss of his "Right Arm" Stonewall Jackson, the North's unrelenting campaign against the South, and with no political and economic recognition from cotton-hungry European nations kept him sleepless. "At Chancellorsville, we gained another victory... our people were wild with delight—I, on the contrary, was more depressed."[20]

The states above the Mason-Dixon Line, by contrast, were well on their way toward a commercial and manufacturing economy, having a direct impact on its war-making ability. By 1860, 90 percent of the nation's manufacturing output came from northern states. The North produced 17 times more cotton and woolen textiles than the South, 30 times more leather goods, 20 times more pig iron, and 32 times more firearms. The North produced 3,200 firearms to every 100 produced in the South. The Massachusetts Springfield Armory Model 1861 produced nearly 140,000 rifles per month.[21] Only about 40 percent of the Northern population was still engaged in agriculture by 1860, as compared to 84 percent of the South."[22] Indeed, the handwriting was on the wall for the South, and Lee knew it. Successes were going to become less in the future. It was a foregone tactical realization to "take the war" to the North and bring the war to a close, and quickly with a decisive blow. Gettysburg was the serendipity for the Union, but the devil for the Confederates.

Bringing the War to the North had multiple confluences in the Rebel arsenal:

a) Morale within the Confederate forces was relatively high; the Union leadership was low as President Lincoln attempted to find a general officer not beset with political machinations.

b) Exploit the unrest in the North. On 3 March 1863, the Union ratified the first involuntary Draft, causing violent hostility

---

[20] Heth, Henry to J. Williams Jones, June 1877, *Southern Historical Society Papers,* Volume 4, pages 153-154; reprint, Millwood, New York: 1977.

[21] "Springfield Model 1861," www.civilwaracademy.com/springfield-model-1861

[22] Arrington, Benjamin T., "Industry and Economy during the Civil War," *National Park Service.* www.nps.gov/articles/industry-and-economy-during-the-civil-war.htm

and upheaval. Lincoln, a week after the battle, diverted several New York, Michigan, and Indiana regiments from Gettysburg to suppress the riots in New York City.[23]

c) Lee needed to resupply the army by foraging the countryside — southern Pennsylvania was ideal — previous raids by Confederate calvary reported back a breadbasket of goods. And, d) capture Pennsylvania's state capitol Harrisburg, a giant railroad marshaling yard and, Camp Curtin, a major military recruiting and training center. Its capture would threaten Philadelphia and isolate the District of Columbia and Baltimore. Pennsylvania's coal fields probably were enticing as well — also the Commonwealth supplied 80 percent of the iron for the federal government.[24] Since the Revolution, Pennsylvania was indeed called the "Keystone State" for sound historical, economic, and political reasons.

Lee's grand strategy invasion would traverse the Shenandoah Valley and its low mountains and entice a disorganized Union army to shadow it northward. The next battle of Lee's choosing would be, in his mind, the *coup de grace* for ending the War.

The invading Confederate soldiers soon learned to dislike the Pennsylvania residents who cursed them for confiscating their bounty despite their ingenuity in hiding such goods. Southcentral Pennsylvania was the agricultural breadbasket of the Keystone State. It was full of provisions, especially when the civilians were quick enough to protect their chattels.

The pre-battle, the June 1863 Rebel pilfering, was tiny because earlier raids prepared the locals who hid their goods.

Rag-clothed from shortages from their homes, the Rebels were "exceedingly dirty, some ragged, some without shoes, and surmounted by the skeleton of what once was an entire hat."[25] The *antebellum* breadbasket of America, the South, was trade blockaded from their northern brethren and foreign trade partners. This hunger at Gettysburg led to the mythological story that Confederate soldiers were after shoes, precipitating an early battle. Instead, they were after everything they could lay their hands upon.

---

[23] 26th Michigan Infantry; 5th, 9th, 17th New York Infantry; 14th Indiana Infantry.

[24] Pennsylvania Historical and Museum Commission. www.phmc.pa.gov/Archives/Research-Online/Pages/Civil-War.aspx

[25] Bloom, Robert L. Emeritus, Gettysburg College. *"We Never Expected a Battle": The Civilians at Gettysburg, 1863*. Gettysburg, Pennsylvania: page 166, quoting resident Michael Jacobs. (An engaging monograph of the civilian prospective of the invasion of Gettysburg, ed.)

WEDNESDAY, 1 JULY 1863, NEAR GETTYSBURG.

The men were dog-tired but excited, rushing to the sound of thunder and cracklings of Buford's cavalry and Hill's infantry. Only two days earlier, they force-marched in the drenching rain to Emmitsburg, Maryland, and camped in the shadow of the Confederate Army.[26] The Army of the Potomac marched from Fredericksburg to the Pennsylvania state line in seven days — 110 miles — remarkable in its day.[27]

"We marched from Frederick City to Emmitsburg, passing on the way through Lewistown, Mechanicstown, and Catoctin Furnace settlement; also passing those famous Catholic institutions of learning, viz, the college and sisterhood near Emmitsburg. Having marched all day in rain and mud, reaching our destination of 23 miles at 5.30 p. m., the men were much fatigued on the march, but all answered and were accounted for at roll-call. We bivouacked about 1 mile west of Emmitsburg and the next day marched to near Gettysburg."[28]

Despite surrendering to the typical hot, humid near-tropical weather of July in south-central Pennsylvania, they were greeted by the civilian population with milk, cakes, pies, making it a celebratory occasion.[29]

Union Major General John Fulton Reynolds, who was from the old school of leading his First Corps troops from the front, arrived around 10 a.m. on the field near East McPherson Ridge near the rustic little town of Gettysburg, the county seat of Adams County, Pennsylvania. "Forward men, forward for God's sake and drive those fellows out of those woods."[30] It was sometime between 10:15-10:45 a.m. Reynolds was fatally struck by a bullet, killing "...not only the highest ranking but also the best general in the army."[31] It was a se-

---

[26] Bates, Samuel Penniman. *History of Pennsylvania Volunteers, 1861-5*; prepared in compliance with acts of the legislature. Harrisburg, Pennsylvania: B. Singerly, State Printer, 1870; Volume 3, page 860.

[27] Guelzo, Allen C. *Gettysburg: The Last Invasion.* New York: Vintage Civil War Library, Vintage Books, 2013, page 117.

[28] Roath, Capt. Emanuel D. "Numbers 51. Report of Captain Emanuel D. Roath, 107th Pennsylvania Infantry." gettysburg.stonesentinels.com/union-monuments/pennsylvania/pennsylvania-infantry/107th-pennsylvania/official-report-for-the-107th-pennsylvania/

[29] Guelzo, page 116.

[30] Gragg, Rod. *The Illustrated Gettysburg Reader: An Eyewitness History of the Civil War's Greatest Battle.* Washington, DC: Regnery History, 2013; pp. 74, 77.

[31] Foote, Shelby. *The Civil War: A Narrative.* Volume 2, Fredericksburg to Meridan. New York: Random House, 1958; page 468.

JOHN FULTON REYNOLDS
Library of Congress

vere blow to the ranks as word passed down about the death of a seasoned soldier's soldier.

Reynolds was a native Pennsylvanian, born in Lancaster in 1820.[32] Nominated in 1837 by then-Senator James Buchanan, he graduated from West Point in 1841, twenty-sixth out of fifty in his class. His first baptism-under-fire came in the Mexican-American War (1846-1848) at the Battles of Monterrey, and Buena Vista, as an

---

[32] Also a distant cousin of the author, 4th cousin, four times re-moved.

artillery officer and promoted for gallantry during those actions. The war was a formative event, shaping lifelong friendships with other officers — some now on the opposite side of the conflict.

Reynold's experience extended into the little known Rogue River Wars (1856), the Utah War with the Mormons (1857-1858), and capping off as Commandant of Cadets at West Point in 1860.

He distinguished himself under several generals during the civil war but was captured in 1862 by an old army colleague now a Confederate General, Daniel Harvey Hill. Reynolds was exchanged for another prisoner a couple of months later. He served admirably under several generals until promoted to major general of volunteers at the end of 1862.

Reportedly asked by President Lincoln to be the next commander of the Army of the Potomac, Reynolds declined. Reynolds personally disliked Lincoln, the political interference and squabbling, all leaving a bad taste for a general officer who preferred to be in the field.

At the beginning of the Gettysburg campaign, Reynolds commanded the First Corps left-wing, the Army of the Potomac, now under the command of George Gordon "Old Snapping Turtle" Meade. Meade, another veteran Pennsylvanian and West Pointer (1831), appointed only three days before the battle to encounter the invasion and had been a subordinate of Reynolds. Meade's early military experience was as a fresh lieutenant in the Corps of Topographical Engineers in the 1840s, which, no doubt served him well grasping the contours of the land, shaping the coming battle to the advantage of his army.

On the first day, Reynolds understood Union Cavalry General John Buford's resistance and the need to preserve the high ground and pushed his men hard. The first day of the battle led to many leadership changes from wounds and deaths. Regiment commander Lt. Col. James McThompson was replaced after being wounded by Captain Emanuel D. Roath. First Brigade commanders Brigadier General Gabriel Renè Paul, critically wounded, was replaced by later wounded Col. Samuel H. Leonard, who was replaced by later wounded and captured Col. Adrian R. Root, who was replaced by Col. Richard Coulter, himself later wounded. The Second Division commander was Brigadier General John Cleveland Robinson. After Reynold's death, the First Corps was commanded by Major General Abner Doubleday.

It was after 2 p.m. when Sergeant William Henry Davis, Jr., and his men of Company E, 107th Pennsylvania Volunteer Infantry Regiment, First Brigade, Second Division, First Corps, Army of the Potomac were moving quickly toward Seminary Ridge. Despite blacksmithing about 40 miles to the West, William never had been to Gettysburg, but he was acquainted with some of its folks and its cottage industries of shoes, tobacco, a college, and seminary.

Company E moved toward the Chambersburg Road and crossed an unfinished railroad cut. "Load your weapons and double quick march," barked down the orders through the ranks from Lt. Col. James McThomson, regiment commander, who brought "... 230 guns and 25 commissioned officers..." into the fight.[33]

The 107th had positioned itself generally in the center of the brigade and at the often historically ignored corner of the "fishhook" of the Union army.

The men reached the foot of Oak Ridge and up the hill, hiding behind a stone fence. When Alfred Iverson's Brigade of the 5th, 12th, 20th, and 23rd North Carolina Infantry Regiments approached, they were surprised by the concealed Union Brigade under Paul. Iverson recollected, "I advanced at once, and soon came in contact with the enemy, strongly posted in woods and behind a concealed stone wall. My brigade advanced to within 100 yards, and a most desperate fight took place."[34] A surprised 500 Confederate soldiers quickly surrendered. A private could have easily turned to Sgt. Davis and exclaimed: *"there's more of them surrendering than us."* The officers ordered the prisoners to the rear, and they continued to secure the low stone wall.

After Iverson's terrible decimation, William's 107th and First Brigade moved up behind the 2nd Brigade in support. It ... "repulsed repeated attacks [principally from the Second Alabama Infantry Regiment] and was engaged until 4 p.m. then retired to Seminary Ridge and constructed Breastworks."[35] With some life still in the 12th North Carolina regiment, it went into a wild charge.[36] It is unclear when William felt a burning sensation in the left hip. Shot while standing, he fell, and his comrades picked him up and carried him off to an ambulance wagon. It was the first piece-of-luck for William:

---

[33] McThomson, Lieutenant Colonel James. "Numbers 50. Report of Lieutenant Colonel James McThomson, 107th Pennsylvania Infantry." gettysburg.stonesentinels.com/union-monuments/pennsylvania/pennsylvania-infantry/107th-pennsylvania/official-report-for-the-107th-pennsylvania/

[34] Iverson, Brig. Gen. Alfred. *Reports of Iverson, C. S. Army, commanding brigade. June 3-August 1, 1863. — The Gettysburg Campaign. Official Record — Series I; -Volume XXVII/2 [S# 44].*

[35] The Battle of Gettysburg, 1st Brigade, 2nd Division, 1st Corps monument citation.

[36] Walter Clark, *Histories of the Several Regiments and Battalions from North Carolina in the Great War 1861-'65.* Goldsboro, North Carolina: Nash Brothers, 1901, Volume 1, page 638.

if left laying on the field, he surely would die. If captured and if he survived, he would languish in a sordid Confederate prison and probably die.

"In his determination to keep open roads to his rear, Meade further complicated supply problems for his medical officers by issuing orders that resulted in hospital supply wagons being kept well back from the battlefield. Most medical officers had to rely entirely on the small medicine wagons that routinely accompanied ambulances in the field."[37]

William was saved by one of these small wagons as he arrived at the field hospital in York rather than in a makeshift hospital in a Gettysburg farmhouse or barn whose injured, for the most part, were left untreated.

Sixty-eight officers and men in the regiment were killed or wounded those few hours. Ninety-three were missing and assumed taken prisoner in the rout. Here, men of the Third Brigade, Second Division, fled to the rear (southeastward) into some woods, throwing up breastworks on Cemetery Hill. The 16th Maine Infantry Volunteers heroically covered the retreat for the brigade and took severe casualties.

In Company E, First Lt. James A. Carman (1831-1864), of Harrisburg, a dentist before the war, was captured during the melee. He would die of yellow fever in prison in Charleston, South Carolina.[38] Artillery Private Henry C. Fahs (1845-1904), also from Harrisburg, and who worked for the railroad, was also wounded.[39] Private George W. Stape (1845-1921), formerly of Lancaster, was also injured the first day. He was shot through the left elbow rendering the arm useless for the rest of his life. Despite his disability, he continued to serve. He was captured and made a prisoner in 1864 and escaped "several Confederate prisons." He eventually was turned over to his compadres during a prisoner exchange. After war he was employed as a battlefield guide at Gettysburg. He was then honored and then interred at the Gettysburg National Cemetery.[40]

Private George B. Wineman (1841-1863), was the only man in the Company killed, but on the last day of the battle, July 3rd, and

---

[37] Gillett, Mary C. *The Army Medical Department 1818-1865*. Washington, D.C: Center of Military History United States Army, 1987, page 211.

[38] "James A. Carman," www.findagrave.com/memorial/51813480

[39] Henry C. Fahs can be found in numerous Harrisburg, Dauphin County, Pennsylvania U.S. Census records, and is buried in the Harrisburg Cemetery with his wife Mary. He also applied for a pension in March 1879. Obituary: 2 February 1904, *Harrisburg Telegraph*, page 9.

[40] Obituary: 23 November 1921, *Gettysburg Times*, page 1.

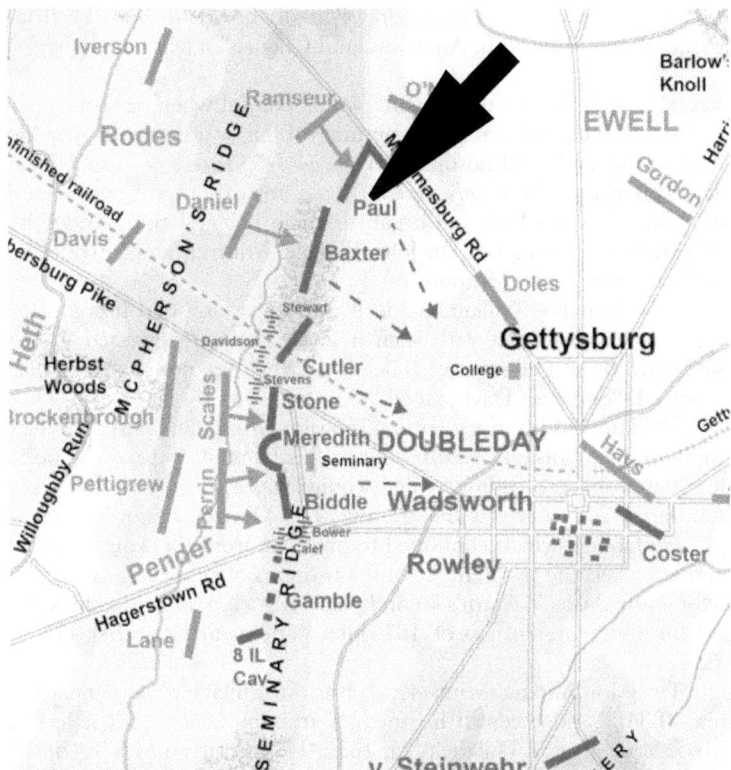

Map by Hal Jespersen, www.posix.com/CW
The arrow points to the area Sgt. Davis was wounded and the important salient of the ridges on the first day of battle.

interred at the Gettysburg National Cemetery. George and William probably knew each other since they were from Path Valley.[41] Sgt. Simon Snyder was captured the first day and released a year later.[42] Lancaster native and Regiment Major Henry Jackson Sheafer (1826-1900) was wounded and discharged a year later. He later became a sheriff of Dauphin County, Pennsylvania.[43] These were the Compa-

---

[41] "Visited His Brother's Grave," *Valley Spirit,* Chambersburg, Franklin County, Pennsylvania, 16 July 1902, page 5.

[42] "Captured at Gettysburg and prisoner from July 1, 1863, to July 3, 1864 - promoted from private on February 28, 1864 - discharged by Special Order on November 20. 1864." www.pacivilwar.com/deaths/gettysburg6.html

[43] Obituary: "Maj. Sheafer Dead," 30 March 1900, *Harrisburg Daily Independent*, Harrisburg, Dauphin County, Pennsylvania, page 1.

ny E casualties at Gettysburg, already badly beaten down prior from battles named Bull Run, Antietam, and Chancellorsville.

William's wound was beyond words painful when he woke up a few hours later, remembering nothing of his wagon trip down the road to the York field hospital. *"Where am I?"* *"You are in a hospital near York, Pennsylvania,"* *an orderly answered* — an answer not unlikely uttered by many. It was a busy but organized field hospital commanded by an experienced surgeon, Dr. John Watkins Mintzer, and it would be William's new home for months.

The fact that William made it into an established hospital for recovery or treatment with such a severe wound suggested to the staff that he might survive. Indeed, a Lancaster newspaper earlier reported, "Sergeant Davis, killed."[44]

William was hit in the left hip, smashing his pelvis, and the bullet went straight through, coming out on his backside with many bone fragments still protruding.[45] The wound was appalling by the day's standards; few survived the trauma. Dr. Mintzer removed several pieces of bone, which continued to protrude from the wound visibly and later became festered; "...and a fistulous opening still exists," he wrote. July 2 was William's second piece of luck, and he was lucky to get the right surgeon out of 167 other patients arriving that Thursday.

Dr. John Watkins Mintzer was born in Philadelphia, Pennsylvania, 1834,[46] and received his medical training at Thomas Jefferson Medical College in Philadelphia, 1850.[47,48] He served as Surgeon of the 26th Pennsylvania Volunteers from June 1861 to March 1863. In March 1863, with deepening concern over the care and organization of medical care for Union soldiers, the US Surgeon Volunteers was organized from input from doctors like him.

Appalled at the medical conditions he observed, he ordered proper sanitation and amended the Surgical Corps administrative records. An experienced surgeon from private practice, he had writ-

---

[44] "List of Killed and Wounded in Company E, 107th Regiment, P. V." *The Inquirer,* Lancaster, Pennsylvania, 6 July 1863, 2nd Edition, page 3.

[45] Surgeon's record.

[46] His death records says born about 1830. "Pennsylvania, Philadelphia City Death Certificates, 1803–1915." Index. www.FamilySearch.org, Salt Lake City, Utah. Originals housed at the Philadelphia City Archives.

[47] Davis, William Watts Hart. *A Genealogical and Personal History of Bucks County, Pennsylvania.* New York, 1905, page 411.

[48] *Catalogue of Jefferson Medical College of Philadelphia Session of 1849-50.* Philadelphia: Frick and Kelly, Printers, 1850, page 8.

Dr. John Watkins Mintzer
American Civil War Medicine & Surgical Antiques, www.medicalantiques.com

ten a report, in June 1862, to the Surgeon General of his experiences and recommendations.[49] Nevertheless, he undoubtedly honed more

---

[49] "A surgeon on the Peninsula: Dr. St. John Watkins Mintzer's report to the Surgeon General, 30 June 1862." *US National Library of Medicine,* National Institutes of Health. www.ncbi.nlm.nih.gov/pubmed/9433116

skills from his regiment's service at the Siege of Yorktown, the Battle of Williamsburg, and various other actions on the Virginia Peninsula. On July 1-3, 1863, he was the Assistant Surgeon in charge of a 1,600-bed field hospital at Penn Common, near York, Pennsylvania, under the tutelage of Dr. Henry Palmer, 7th Wisconsin Infantry. Dr. Palmer was a Brigadier Surgeon of the U.S. Volunteers since 1861 and received his training at Albany [New York] Medical College in 1854. The hospital in York served over 14,000 patients and had one of the lowest mortality rates of any Union hospital.

"[The] hospital is simply a piece of ground in the form of a square containing perhaps 20 acres & bounded on two sides by a double row of one story buildings & on the other 2 by a high and close board fence & was originally designed & used for a camp ground & barracks for soldiers ... The rooms are low ill ventilated, there is not a tree or bush on the ground & the number of seats outside the buildings is [very] small ... There is a post office & small

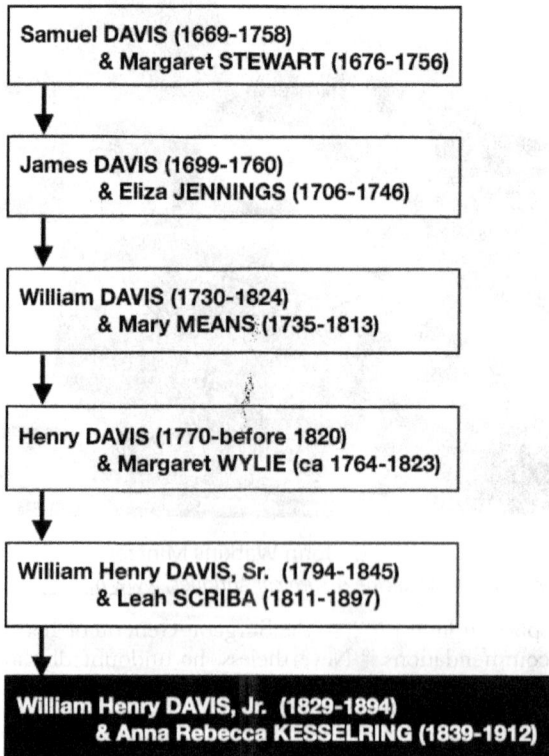

```
┌─────────────────────────────────────────────┐
│   Samuel DAVIS (1669-1758)                    │
│       & Margaret STEWART (1676-1756)          │
└─────────────────────────────────────────────┘
                    │
                    ▼
┌─────────────────────────────────────────────┐
│   James DAVIS (1699-1760)                     │
│       & Eliza JENNINGS (1706-1746)            │
└─────────────────────────────────────────────┘
                    │
                    ▼
┌─────────────────────────────────────────────┐
│   William DAVIS (1730-1824)                   │
│       & Mary MEANS (1735-1813)                │
└─────────────────────────────────────────────┘
                    │
                    ▼
┌─────────────────────────────────────────────┐
│   Henry DAVIS (1770-before 1820)              │
│       & Margaret WYLIE (ca 1764-1823)         │
└─────────────────────────────────────────────┘
                    │
                    ▼
┌─────────────────────────────────────────────┐
│   William Henry DAVIS, Sr. (1794-1845)        │
│       & Leah SCRIBA (1811-1897)               │
└─────────────────────────────────────────────┘
                    │
                    ▼
┌─────────────────────────────────────────────┐
│   William Henry DAVIS, Jr. (1829-1894)        │
│       & Anna Rebecca KESSELRING (1839-1912)   │
└─────────────────────────────────────────────┘
```

soldiers library on the grounds ... Every man who is considered well enough can obtain a pass to go into town once in 3 days between the hours of 1 & 5 p.m."[50]

Building the Penn Park army hospital began 9 June 1862, converting an old barracks erected the last winter by the 6th New York Cavalry.[51] The hospital, especially after the mass casualties from the Battle of Antietam, September 1862, expanded and became the largest military field hospital during the conflict. It seems William was in better hands than most.

BEFORE GETTYSBURG

William's mind probably drifted off to the cold wintery day in late January 1862 at the kitchen table of his home in Guildford Township, Franklin County, Pennsylvania, having left Horse Valley. His wife, Anna Rebecca *nee* Kesselring, was 23 years of age with three daughters all under four years of age — the last one born a few days before preparing to report for induction. The conversation at the kitchen table was not too imaginary:

"Why do you want to enlist in the Army and for three years?" Anna asked with apprehension and fear.

"We discussed this already."

"Yep, and I never thought it was a great idea. It's sure and fine for you to go off, leaving me behind with small children and a household to take care of."

Perhaps it was duty or opportunity or both for William.

Thirteen months previously, South Carolina seceded from the Union; three months later, the Confederate States of America formed, and a month after that formation, Abraham Lincoln became the 16th President of the United States, igniting the civil war to come. In April 1861, nine months before William and Ann's kitchen discussion, Fort Sumter was fired upon, and Lincoln in April 1861, asked for 75,000 militiamen to be raised. Seeing the defeat of federal troops at Bull Run, 21 July 1861, Lincoln asked for more men to suppress the rebellion. William, no doubt, read the papers of the disastrous rout. It was this call for 500,000 "Three Year Men" that William eventually answered.

"Traitors. That's who we are fighting, Ann. My folks have been in this country since the 1600s and fought in the Revolution for one nation — not two. That's why I want to go. After Sumter, I thought it would be all over. The South-

---

[50] Smith, James M. *Letter*. 25 July 1863, Company G, 149th New York Infantry. New York State Library.

[51] "A Government Hospital At York," *York Gazette*, York, York County, Pennsylvania, 10 June 1862, page 2.

ern states don't have many men. Then there was Bull Run — I knew the 'cess folks would last longer in their fight. I didn't go into the army then because Mac wasn't in charge. But since he is in charge now, I'm inclined to go. Besides that, Ann, I'm 32 years old and we are still dirt poor. I've tried making a living here under the graces of my father and taking up blacksmithing with your father, and getting along with your family. You know they don't like me."

"They are upset with me too, but it's been nearly five years since our marriage," confirmed Anna. (Not a documented conversation, but no doubt a likely one that took place in many kitchens.)

William and Ann were married on 1 August 1857 in Path Valley, in Franklin County, near the home she was born in Path Valley. She was 16, and he was 28 years of age. Anna inherited her stubbornness from her ancestral German father and Irish mother and married William against her father's wishes. Things were rough between her and the family. Her father, John Kesselring, 47 years old, alive and well, was a successful blacksmith. Now, a neighbor just down the road, in the marriage record, Ann stated: "I don't know who my parents are." Father John had recently re-married a year before to Catherine Laidig. Rebecca's biological mother, Susanna Hawk nee Delaney, passed away three years prior at 38. Susan's father, James Delaney, Jr., was also a blacksmith and a namesake to his father, who had married Rebecca Cerfass. James Delaney, Sr., was a reported runaway indentured servant from Ireland and enlisted in the American Revolutionary Army as part of his escape. He married Mary Vanderbilt, a third cousin to financial tycoon Cornelius Vanderbilt. However, the shirt-tale relationship never enjoyed any of that prosperity.

Judging by his neighbor's wealth, William was not making it financially.[52] In his defense, his older male relatives were well established and successful from time in the trade and age.

William's father, William Henry Davis, Senior (1794-1845), a blacksmith, came from a long line of Scot-Irish Presbyterian stalwarts. William Senior was involved in the 1840 presidential campaign reported by son James Vanlear Davis who found the Whig campaign button of his father.[53] The Whig National Convention was first held in Harrisburg in 1839 then in Baltimore in 1840. The Whigs asserted that the federal government's powers were paramount when state powers were not enumerated in the Constitution

---

[52] "1860 United States Census," National Archives and Records Administration (NARA). M653, Roll 1112, Metal Township, Franklin County, Pennsylvania; Page 577. Value of Real Estate: $450; Personal value: $350.

[53] *Public Opinion,* Chambersburg, Franklin County, Pennsylvania, 5 October 1888, page 1.

and believed in an interventionist economic system favoring internal infrastructure improvement. This often hazy political view would influence the family as a cultural overview of participation in the community. William's mother was Leah Scriba, daughter of an itinerant Lutheran minister and immigrant from German-speaking Europe, Rev. Wilhelm Heindrich Scriba (1768-1840).

William Senior's father, Henry Davis (1770-died before 1820), was a Revolutionary War soldier married to Margaret Wylie (ca 1764-1823). Henry's father was William Davis (1730-1824), born in County Tyrone, Ireland, and a Revolutionary War soldier married to Mary Means (1735-1813). William immigrated to The Colonies with his father, James Davis (1699-1760), and family in 1735 to the Bucks County, Pennsylvania area. James also served in the militia military as a Lieutenant during the tumultuous 1748-1748 King George's War on the frontier with the French and native Indians. James was married to another Scot-Irish Presbyterian from northern Ireland Eliza Jennings (1706-1746). James had immigrated to America with his father and mother William Davis (1669-1758) and Margaret Stewart (1676-1756).[54]

But like most families of the era, wife Anna would not have to shoulder most of the work. There were plenty of relatives on both sides to go around to help her out. By the time of husband William's enlistment, they had three young daughters:

i.   Leah Susan (1858-1888); later married Charles Henry Lippy
ii. Ida Ellen (1860-1932); married John Henry Rudolph
iii. Mary Jane (1862-1922); married Benjamin Franklin Hetrick

THE WAR HOOPLA

But for the Civil War, William believed he was doing his patriotic duty and running on the fumes of ancestry to save the Union, and the sentiment was high from folks in his area. After the firing upon Fort Sumter, local militia groups were forming up. In nearby county Adams, the "Union Rifle" militia formed with new blue uniforms "...very neat and attractive."[55] In April 1861, Pennsylvania's Governor, Andrew Curtin, demanded "...$500,000 to place this State on a War Footing"[56] as well as urging a military commission in defense of

---

[54] All faithfully recorded by Rev. Thomas Kirby Davis. *The Davis Family Book, A History of the Descendants of William Davis and his Wife, Mary Means.* Norwood, Massachusetts: The Plimpton Press, 1912.

[55] "New Company," *The Adams Sentinel,* newspaper, Gettysburg, Adams County, Pennsylvania, 16 January 1861, page 2.

[56] "Gov. Curtin's Standing Army," *The Valley Spirit,* 17 April 1861, page 4.

the Commonwealth. In nearby Chambersburg, county-seat of William's home county Franklin, the "Chambers Artillery," a 50-man infantry company, mustered with one brass six-pounder cannon accompanied by the "Mechanics' Brass Band," who swaggered their talent in the newspapers and backyards of the locals. An active militia since 1858, it was given a shot of new purpose joining with the "St. Thomas Artillery."[57] These volunteers of three companies left for Harrisburg becoming part of the 2nd Pennsylvania Volunteers in April 1861.[58] "The military will be out on the occasion and the Band in attendance and enliven the event by playing our national airs in their best style."[59] "The Chambers Artillery was uniformed in long dark blue frock coats and trousers... The trimmings and rank insignia were regulation red. The chapeau was a high fancy shape, high crowned, red hat band with a white plume."[60]

This initial war hoopla made only a cautious William. A husband with a young wife and three small children, he apparently remained uncommitted and silent.

But after the disastrous engagement at Bull Run, it wouldn't be all marching bands, pleasant feelings, and fancy parade uniforms. William was reading the scrawl in the local newspapers. It was just a matter of time that more men from the area would join up from peer pressure and financial reasons, and later The Draft.

His brother-in-law George A. Miller (1834-1885), who married to his sister Rebecca Elizabeth Davis (1838-1910), joined the 126th Regiment, Pennsylvania Volunteers, Company G in August 1862.

William's brother, James Vanlear Davis (1833-1900), would register with the Draft of 1863 but never mustered into service.

William's other brother, Robert Cunningham Davis (1843-1882), was the first to join up in the family with the 41st Regiment of Pennsylvania Volunteer Infantry, possibly influencing William's decision. Robert joined in June 1861 as a headquarters clerk. He was taken prisoner a year later but paroled a few months after — only to be shot in the forearm in December 1862 at Fredricksburg, Virginia. The surgeon did not amputate but was transferred to the invalid corps and served as a hospital steward. Brother-in-law, Samuel Allison Gamble (1834-1912), married to sister Mary Ellen Davis

[57] "Flag Presentation," *The Shippensburg News,* newspaper, Shippensburg, Cumberland County, Pennsylvania, 11 June 1859, page 1.

[58] "Rebel Firing on Fort Sumter...," *Public Opinion*, 10 April 1961, page 9

[59] "The War Feeling." *The Valley Spirit,* 17 April 1861, page 4.

[60] "First Defenders Here in Civil War Subject of Paper," *Public Opinion*, 27 November 1926, page 3.

(1840-1915), joined the cause after the Burning of Chambersburg, July 1864, with Company I, 201st Pennsylvania Volunteer Infantry.

William finally signed his mark on the enlistment papers, 15 November 1861, despite his wife seven months pregnant with their third child and daughter. Perhaps the instigation came a few days earlier, 8 November, when the U.S. Navy seized a ship with two Confederate envoys to England. England protested, threatening war. For pragmatic reasons, the Confederates were released: "one war at a time," Lincoln remarked. But the incident was enough for William's pent-up patriotism. He signed up with Company B, 107th Infantry Regiment Pennsylvania Volunteers as a Private, mustered in 6 February 1862. Described five feet, eight inches tall, dark complexed, blue eyes, black hair, he made his mark on the enlistment papers (despite being literate). He left his family and traveled to Chambersburg, taking the Pennsylvania Railroad[61] train to Harrisburg, and disembarking at Camp Curtin — a military training center named after wartime Pennsylvania Governor Andrew Gregg Curtin. Camp Curtin was a major "boot" hub of soldiers ideally placed within Harrisburg's numerous railway lines coming to the capital city of Pennsylvania. "Over 300,000 soldiers passed through Camp Curtin," making it the largest Federal camp during the Civil War,"[62] "...on 80 acres of land from the County Agricultural Society, ...more military units were organized here than ... any other Northern camp."[63]

Shortly after that, William was mustered into Company I of the 107th regiment of Pennsylvania Volunteer Infantry, as a private, under Capt. MacThompson.

Earlier, in the fall of 1861, a soldier/veteran of the Mexican War, Thomas A. Zeigle of York County and Robert W. McAllen of Franklin County, were given the authority to form a regiment, occurring on 5 March 1862, formally granted its colors at Harrisburg. The regimental flag was a regulation size 34-star national color with the state coat-of-arms painted in the blue canton with "107th Regt. P.V." in the center red stripe. The regiment consisted of groups of men from various counties:

---

[61] The railroad line from Chambersburg to Harrisburg was well established under the Cumberland Valley Railroad in 1837. The Pennsylvania Railroad took over management in 1859 and was a target of the Confederates in the October 1862 Raid on Chambersburg, actions before the Battle of Gettysburg, June 1863 and the Burning of Chambersburg, July 1864.

[62] Camp Curtin. en.wikipedia.org/wiki/Camp_Curtin

[63] Camp Curtin Historical Society, P.O. Box 5601, Harrisburg, Pennsylvania 17110. www.campcurtin.org

- Company A: Luzerne and York counties
- Company B: Berks, Cumberland and Franklin counties
- Company C: Lycoming, Sullivan and Wyoming counties
- Company D: Mifflin and Schuylkill counties
- Company E: Juniata and Lancaster counties
- Company F: various counties
- Company G: Bradford and Schuylkill counties
- Company H: Franklin and Fulton counties as well as others
- Company I: Lebanon and multiple counties
- Company K: various counties

The 107th regiment did not have enough men at its formation on 7 March 1862 and probably why William was later set out on recruitment duties. There were strong prejudices at the beginning of the war: "The men we have are principally Americans, a few Germans. We could get three companies of Irish but will not have them unless we are forced to take them."[64]

William went through boot camp like all the others and finally was issued the Austrian Lorenz Rifle, a .54 caliber, percussion cap muzzleloading rifle-musket.[65] His muster card of April 1862, shows him transferred to Captain Emanuel D. Roath, of Harrisburg, on the previous March 1. For reasons unknown, he was then promoted to Sergeant, 30 January 1862, and enrolled and transferred in Company E of the regiment. The newly minted Sergeant Davis was "encamped near Washington, D. C." as a fourth sergeant for the company.[66]

Promotion came perhaps because he was an older man of 34 years, had worked his own business, was a skilled blacksmith, or they just plain liked him. A piece of luck: they put him on recruiting duty — perhaps he had skills at persuasion too. It would not be easy recruitment duty: the war was immensely unpopular in the Northern states. Sergeant Davis's recruitment duties took him to various places as a member of the Permanent Recruitment Party, according to his muster records:

- May and June 1862: Dushore, Pa.
- September and October 1862: Shippensburg, Cumberland County, Pennsylvania.

---

[64] Thomas, Mary Warner, *et al*; page 25; James Belcombe Thomas, Adjutant, 107th regiment, 6 December 1861.

[65] Ibid.; page 29.

[66] "Muster Roll of Capt. E. D. Roath's Company E, 107th Regiment, P. V.," *Lancaster Intelligencer,* newspaper, Lancaster, Lancaster County, Pennsylvania, 1 April 1862, page 2.

- 30 June to 31 October 1862: Detailed on recruiting party.
- November and December 1862: Nicholson, Wyoming County, Pennsylvania.
- January and February 1863: Detailed on recruiting service, 28 June 1862.

Recruitment must have been a tough sell by mid-1863. Desertions in the army were "...200 a day by one estimate, and over 25,000 by the end of January" 1863.[67] "...[T]he Civil War volunteer was a temporary soldier, long on self-esteem and very, very short on experience."[68]

His recruitment duties abruptly ended with the institution of the unpopular Draft registration, passed by Congress in March 1863. No need for a recruiter when you can extract "boots" from the general populace by force of law.

It is unclear if Sergeant Davis participated in the Battle of Chancellorsville, 30 April to 6 May 1863 in Spotsylvania County, Virginia. His muster roll of May and June 1863 simply shows him "present." He was, never-the-less, unscathed by the experience, which would have been his first taste of combat and integration with soldiers not from his home county, and new to him. The regiment participated in actions at nearby Pollock's Mill Creek, and Fitzhugh's Crossing, 29 April - 2 May.[69] Williams regiment saw little action, crossing the south side of the Rappahannock River 1 May[70] and capturing some prisoners. "Nothing of interest occurred until evening of 30th [April] when the enemy opened several batteries [sic] on us."[71] The regiment, on the extreme left of the Union deployment of the battle, posted vedettes and dug trenches. They encountered light skirmishes.

GOING HOME

After the Battle of Gettysburg, William's languishment continued at the York hospital until November 1863, when he transferred

---

[67] Guelzo, page 30.

[68] Ibid. page 11.

[69] Dyer, Frederick H. *A Compendium of the War of the Rebellion.* Des Moines, Iowa: 1908; reprinted 1979 The Press of Morningstar Bookshop, Dayton, Ohio. Volume 2, page 1610.

[70] Reynolds, John F., *Major-General of Volunteers, Commanding; May 1863; Itinerary of the Corps, April 19-May 26. April 27-May 6, 1863.--The Chancellorsville Campaign. Official Record* Series I, Volume XXV/1 [S# 39] civilwarhome.com/reynoldschancellorsvilleor.html

[71] Thomas, *et al*, page 163.

to the post-hospital in Chambersburg. It was closer to home. A pension record summary indicated he deserted 6 January 1864 but was readmitted three days later — apparently with no repercussions.[72] He remained there until March 1864 when his muster showed him back again at York hospital, where he was discharged 24 October 1864 by Dr. Mintzer. "I certify, that I have carefully examined the said Sergeant William H. Davis… and find him incapable of performing the duties of a soldier…" thus becoming one of the official 51,000 plus Union and Confederate casualties of the three-day battle.[73]

William was officially mustered-out 13 July 1865 after Lee's surrender at Appomattox Court House, and Lincoln's assassination in April. The war was near end.

William "recovered" from his war wound eventually, but never to work in his blacksmithing trade again. After a year at home, his wife gave birth to:

iv.   William Scriba Davis (1866-1902), his first son, who later married Bertha M. Embick, and

v.   Caroline Bell Davis (1868-1895).

By 1870, just over 40 years of age, he worked as a farm laborer and had no real estate and minimal personal property value of $250, much lower than the national standard.[74] He had moved out of Horse Valley, closer to Chambersburg, renting farmland from relatives. His only avenue for work was farming. It was taxing on an old, disabled man with a shattered pelvis.

By June 1880,[75] the whole family had moved into Chambersburg, onto Water Street. Including himself, William, now over 50 years of age, had ten souls under his roof. More correctly, under the roof of Waldo and Maggie Curtis with whom they resided as renters. He picked up odd-jobs as a "laborer" to support the family.

---

[72] Desertions on both sides of the conflict was common problem. Soldiers who returned on their own volition were usually ignored for punishment — especially if they lived nearby or were wounded. The term can be loosely compared as "Absent-Without-Official-Leave" (AWOL), a term used in the 20th century.

[73] Casualties at Gettysburg vary per source but all come within 5% of 23,049 for the Union (3,155 dead, 14,529 wounded, 5,365 missing). Confederate casualties were 28,063 (3,903 dead, 18,735 injured, and 5,425 missing), more than a third of Lee's army. https://www.historynet.com/battle-of-gettysburg

[74] "1870 United States Census," Guilford Township, Franklin County, Pennsylvania; NARA M593, Roll 1345, page 236A.

[75] "1880 United States Census," Chambersburg, Franklin County, Pennsylvania; NARA T9, Roll 1132, Family 203; Page 26B.

Anna and William Davis, circa 1880s.
(Karen Sue Eberly/Beth Ann Thomas Powers)

Between 1870 and 1880 were born:

vi.   James Lawrence (1871-1871)
vii. Bertus Eberly (1872-1945); later married Ida Jane Doner
viii. John Robert (1874-1874)
ix.   Charles Henry (1875-1890)
x.   Thomas Elmer (1878-1940); married Ida May Embich
xi.   Hettie Virginia (1880-1904); married Edward Berger

Those years were filled with some grief: two sons had died in infancy.

In 1880, the wealth of the family was not measured, but everyone was pitching into work. Wife Anna and daughter Leah were keeping-up the house; Mary was working at a paper mill, son William Scriba was working at a brickyard. Caroline and Bertus were in school. Charles, Thomas, and Hettie were all under age five.

Daughter Leah married Charles Henry Lippy in 1881. Leah, disabled with rheumatism, died in 1888, after drinking a lethal potion for her illness in 1888; an untimely early death at age 30.

37

The adventuresome daughter Ida Ellen was somewhere out west seeking her fortune. In 1881, she married to a German immigrant, John Henry Rudolph (1850-1929), in Colorado. They later moved to California, and according to family lore, were relatively well-off and helped the extended family financially during the Depression Era from proceeds of a silver mine they owned in Colorado.[76]

Daughter Mary Jane, was out of the house and married to Benjamin Franklin "Frank" Hetrick, around 1880.

In February 1884, William became the "...keeper of the gate west of the Point Hotel..."[77] The income was sufficient for him to erect a two-story frame house, 20 by 24, in Hamilton Township.[78] Not letting his civic duties pass, he was elected Justice of the Peace, Hamilton Township in 1886 by three votes,[79] but lost the election in 1887.[80]

Also, in July 1887, he was present with 40 other 107th veterans at Gettysburg to locate the sites a monument and two markers to be erected in 1888.[81]

Not to let his life be dull, William was thrown from a buggy driven by John Shatzer and broke his leg racing to the funeral of Jacob Snider. Shatzer and Snider were veterans of the 126th regiment — the same regiment William's brother-in-law George Miller was a member of. Both teams were going rapidly after turning a corner and were surprised by another wagon. William's leg required medical attention.[82]

On 9 July 1890, he applied for an Invalid Pension being unable to earn support because of "Hemorrahage of Lungh." Pulmonary bleeding from the lungs could describe many ailments. Still, in the 19th century, it could be confidently diagnosed as "consumption" or tuberculosis — the leading cause of death at that time along, with pneumonia.[83] He was granted the pension at a rate of $4 a month.

---

[76] Confirmed by her great-niece, Helen Mae Davis Sanders, to the author, circa 1968.

[77] "Change of Toll-Gate Keepers." *The Valley Spirit,* 27 February 1884, page 3.

[78] "In All The House." *The Valley Spirit*, 23 December 1885, page 3.

[79] Ibid., 24 February 1886, page 2.

[80] Ibid., 23 February 1887, page 1.

[81] Ibid. 28 July 1887, page 3.

[82] "Leg Broken at a Funeral." *Public Opinion*, 29 August 1888, page 1, 2.

[83] The Center for Disease Control, Atlanta, Georgia. "Achievements in Public Health, 1900-1999: Control of Infectious Diseases," *Morbidity and Mortality Weekly Report.* July 30, 1999; 48(29); pages 621–629.

The 1890 Special "Veterans" census says little about William or the family.[84] His son Charles Henry Davis, disabled from hip disease, was killed that September in a freak accident when a tree fell on him when he couldn't escape fast enough.[85] With the death of his son Charles, his sicknesses, employed as a toll-keeper on the Lincoln Highway west of Chambersburg, the burdens of age weighed upon William and Anna.

Death finally numbered William at 64, and he passed away, 29 March 1894, at his home in Hamilton Township. Stricken with paralysis for some days, he never rallied back and a second stroke captured his soul.[86]

"William H. Davis, the well-known gatekeeper on the Chambersburg and Bedford turnpike, west of this place, died yesterday morning, after a brief illness from paralysis. Mr. Davis was a native of Letterkenny township, but resided in Fannettsburg for a number of years. Since the late war he has been a resident of Chambersburg and vicinity, and for a great many years has been the trustworthy gate-keeper of the turnpike Company.

He was a gallant soldier of the war for the suppression of the rebellion, and was severely wounded at the battle of Gettysburg. he was a member of the 107th Pennsylvania volunteers. In his death Housum Post loses one of its most active and useful members. He is survived by a wife and family, and Jas. V. Davis, of Fannettsburg, was his brother. The funeral will take place on Sunday at 2 p. m. Interment in Cedar Grove cemetery.

Mr. Davis was in the 65th [sic] year of his age."[87,88]

---

[84] 1890 US Special Census Schedule. — Surviving Soldiers, Sailors, and Marines, and Widows, etc. [of the Civil War]; NARA M123; Enumeration District 149; Line 34; House 187; Family 198; Franklin County, Pennsylvania.

[85] "Instantly Killed. A Falling Tree Crushes out the Life of Charley Davis," *Public Opinion,* 11 September 1890, page 3, and 12 September 1890, page 5.

[86] *Harrisburg Telegraph,* newspaper, Harrisburg, Dauphin County, Pennsylvania. 29 March 1894, page 1.

[87] "The Well-Known Gate-Keeper, Wm. H. Davis, Passes Away." *Public Opinion,* 30 March 1894, page 5.

[88] "THE 'SPIRIT'S' NECOLOGICAL LIST: Franklin County People Who Have Been Summoned to Another World." *The Valley Spirit,* 4 April 1894, page 7.

Dr. Mintzer, who patched him up 31 years earlier, passed away in December of that year, in Philadelphia, from throat cancer.[89]

After William's death his widow, Ann, filed for a pension on 4 April 1894:

"Declaration for Widow's Pension. State of Pennsylvania, County of Franklin, ss:

On this 4 day of April, A. D. one thousand eight hundred and ninety four personally appeared before me, a clerk of the Quarter Sessions Court within and for the county and State aforesaid Ann R. Davis, aged 54 years, a resident of the Twp of Hamilton, county of Franklin, State of Penna, who, being duly sworn according to law, declares that she is the widow of William H. Davis, who enlisted under the name of William H. Davis, at Harrisburg Pa on the 6th day of February, A. D. 186[2], in Sgt. in Co. E. 107 Pa. Inftry Vols. and served at least ninety days in the late War of Rebellion, in the service of the United States, who was honorably discharged 24 Oct. 1864, and died Mch. 29, 1894. That she was married under the name of Ann R. Kesselring to said William H. Davis on the 11 day of August, 1856, by Rev. West, at Path Valley Pa., there being no legal barrier to said marriage. There was no prior marriages by either the soldier of claimant. That she has not remarried since the death of the said William H. Davis. That she is without other means of support than her daily labor; that names and dates of birth of all the children now living under sixteen years of age of the soldier are as follows:

Hettie V., born April 21, 1880.

That she makes this declaration for the purpose of being place on the pension-roll of the United States under the provisions of the Act of June 27, 1890.

She appoints with full power of substitution and revocation, George W. Atherton, of Chambersburg State of Penn's, her true and lawful attorney to prosecute her claim, and to receive therefore a fee of ten dollars; that her post-office address is Chambersburg county of Franklin, State of Pa.

Ann R Davis

Attest: David S. Parker, William Rankins

---

89 "Catahar of the Throat." "Dr. Mintzer's Death," The *Philadelphia Times,* newspaper, Philadelphia, Pennsylvania, 29 December 1894, page 7; says he was 64 years of age. However, his Philadelphia Death Certificate says death was in Philadelphia and born 1830, other sources say Bucks County. Enlistment record suggest born 1833; his tombstone says born in 1834. The newspaper obituary says death from "cancer" but his pension records are more specific.

Also personally appeared David S. Parker residing at Housum, Pa, and William Rankins, residing at Housum Pa, persons whom I certify to be respectable and entitled to credit, and who, being by me duly sworn, say that they were present and saw Ann R. Davis, the claimant, sign her name (or make her mark) to the foregoing declaration; that they have every reason to believe from the appearance of said claimant and an acquaintance with her of 10 years and 5 years, respectively, that she is the identical person she represent herself to be, and that they have no interest in the prosecution of this claim.

David S. Parker

William Rankins

Sworn to and subscribed before me this 4 day of April A. D. 1894; and I hereby certify that the contents of the above declaration, &c., were fully made known and explained to the applicant and witnesses before swearing, including the words [blank] erased and the words [blank] added, and that I have no interest, direct or indirect, in the prosecution of this claim.

D. L. Grove, Clerk Quarter Sess Court"

"26 April 1894: General Affidavit. State of Pennsylvania, County of Franklin, ss:

In the matter of the claim of Ann R. Davis widow of William H. Davis of Co. E. 107 Pa Vols. Personally came before me a [blank] in and for aforesaid County and State S. S. Reicher aged 51 years and David Reasoner aged 63 years citizen of the Town of Chambersburg County Franklin State of Pa well known to me to be reputable and to be entitled to credit, and who being duly sworn, declare in relation to aforesaid case as follows: We both knew the claimant and her late husband at least ten years. He owned no real estate and not much personal property. He had a horse and cow and a couple of old wagons and his household goods. We do not believe that all the property he left is worth more than $300. The claimant has not money or property except what her husband left.

She has not remarried since the soldiers death.

The above statement was prepared for her in our presence by G W Atherton of Chambersburg Pa April 26, 1890, and in making the same we did not use nor were not aided by any recital or written or printed memory card.

They further declare that they have no interest in said case, and are not concerned in its prosecution.

Saml. Reicher, David Reasoner"

24 July 1894: General Affidavit from widow Ann R. Davis, age 54, Chambersburg, Franklin County, Pennsylvania:

"I am the claimant. My husband was in no other service before or since his service in Co. E. 107 Pa Inf. My husbanded not own any real estate, and I do not own any real estate. The personnel property he left me is one horse 2 cowes 2 old wagons and an old buggy, and a few household goods. The value of the whole of them I doubt if it is more than $300. No body is legally bound to support me. I have no income at all. This statement is made to G W Atherton [attorney] at Chambersburg Pa July 24, 1894. He preformed the form in my presence, and in making the form I was not aided by any [illegible] or written or printer [illegible]."

She was granted that pension by February 1895.[90]

Several events, serious and gossipy interrupted her widowed and retired tranquility:

• November 1895, her 28-year-old daughter Carrie Davis died at her mother's home at the tollgate.[91]

• In May 1896, her uncle James Cerfass Delaney paid her and the family a visit from his domicile in Green Bay, Wisconsin.[92] That August, her granddaughter, Ruth Hetrick, died from "dropsy" at her home at age 15 years.[93]

• Granddaughter Mary Belle Lippy, age 16, died in June, 1900.[94]

• In December 1901, her son William Scriba Davis passed away from consumption at his home. Only a few years earlier, in 1898, in a sensational fire, he narrowly escaped burning to death after setting his house on alight after laying his pipe down after falling asleep. The house burned to the ground.[95]

• Her daughter, Hattie Virginia Davis, died in 1904 from consumption, age 24.[96]

---

[90] "Jottings...," *People's Register,* newspaper, Chambersburg, Franklin County, Pennsylvania, 1 February 1895, page 1.

[91] *Valley Spirit,* 6 November 1895, page 5.

[92] "Personal Matters Noted for Our Readers' Information," *Public Opinion,* 7 May 1896, page 2.

[93] "Death List." *Public Opinion,* 15 August 1896, page 3.

[94] *Valley Spirit,* 20 June 1900, page 7.

[95] *Shippensburg News,* Shippensburg, Pennsylvania, 15 July 1898, page 2 and "Davis' Costly Smoke," *Valley Spirit,* 6 July 1898, page 1. "This Was a Costly Smoke," *Public Opinion,* 8 July 1898, page 5; 12 July 1898, page 2. "Local and General" *The Compiler,* newspaper, Gettysburg, Adams County, Pennsylvania, 12 July 1898, page 2. *The Gazette,* newspaper, York, York County, Pennsylvania, 7 July 1898, page 4. "Cumberland Valley," *Daily Telegraph,* newspaper, Harrisburg, *Dauphin County, Pennsylvania, 8 July 1898, page 2. Obituary,* Valley Spirit, 4 December 1901, page 5.

[96] "Davis." *People's Register,* 14 October 1904, page 5.

- By 1894, Anna obtained some property in Letterkenny Township, living near "Keefer's Store." A gossipy newspaper iota reported her securing three pumpkins, the largest weighing 115 pounds.[97]
- In 1905 her tranquility was shattered by the sensationalized death of her depressed, unemployed, son-in-law Frank Hetrick, who drank a lethal dose of an opiate derived concoction.[98]
- In November 1910, her grandson Bertous Davis Hetrick, 23, died in an accidental fall, while working as an electrical lineman.[99]
- Poverty led her to sell her only cow and a "…lot of Household Goods, etc." in September, 1911.[100]

Alas, 7 February 1912, Anna met her eternal rest at 15 High Street, Chambersburg, age 72 years.[101]

"Mrs. Anna R. Davis. Aged 72 Years

Mrs. Anna R., widow of W. H. Davis, who formerly kept the tollgate north of town, died Wednesday night at her home, 15 High street, aged 72 years, 2 months and 11 days. She is survived by the following children: Mrs. Ida Rudolph of Sandiago, [sic] Cal.; Mrs. Jennie Hetrick of Chambersburg; B. E. Davis of Hamilton township; Thomas E. Davis of Chambersburg. Twenty-three grand children and three great grandchildren also survive, as do a sister and two brothers: Mrs. James McDonald of Colorado; Lewis Kesseling of Colorado and Leonard Kesseling of Fulton county.

Funeral services on Saturday at 2 p. m., Revs. T. A. Alspach and F. L. Bergstresser officiating. Interment in Cedar Grove cemetery."[102]

A few months later, on 5 June 1912: "Pensioner Dropped. Pensioner Ann R. Davis. Certificate number 406319. 'SIR: I have the honor to report that the above-named pensioner who was last paid at $12 to Jan. 4 - 1912 has been dropped because of death Feby 7 - 1912.'"

Earlier, in February 1912, Anna's son Thomas Elmer Davis was named the executor of her Last Will Testament. "A public sales was ordered of Real Estate."

---

[97] "Some Jumbo Pumpkins," *People's Register,* 3 November 1905, page 1.

[98] "Frank Hetrick…" *Valley Spirit,* 13 September 1905, page 2.

[99] "Lineman Killed in Fall From Roof," *The Gazette,* York, Pennsylvania, 19 November 1910, page 9.

[100] "Public Sale of Personal Property," *People's Register,* 1 September 1911, page 4.

[101] "Mrs. Anna R. Davis." *The Valley Spirit,* 9 February 1912, page 5 and 14 February 1912, page 3.

[102] *Public Opinion,* 8 February 1912, pages 1, 3.

"Saturday, Sept, 14, 1912. House and lot containing about two acres, situate in Letterkenny Township, Franklin County, Pa., near Karper's Church, bounded by lands formerly of Wm. S. Keefer, John H. Huber's heirs, et al. Improvements, weatherboard house containing 5 rooms, wash house, frame stale and other needed out buildings. Fruit of different kinds on the premises. Well of good water at the door and cistern at the house. A desirable home convenient to store, school and church... B[ertus] E[berly] Davis, Executor... [her son]."[103]

All the surviving children divided up the small estate. The final account of her estate published in 1913.[104]

The Commonwealth of Pennsylvania finally honored William Henry Davis, Jr. with his other fellow 34,530 Pennsylvanians who fought at Gettysburg when the Pennsylvania State Memorial was completed by 1914. His name, placed upon the wall with the regiment.

---

[103] "Public Sale of Real Estate," *People's Register,* 16 August 1912, page 4; 23 August 1912, page 4; 30 August 1912, page 4; 6 September 1912, page 4; 13 September 1912, page 4. (Previous "Executor's Notice" published 2 March 1912, page 4; 11 March 1912, page 4; 16 March 1912, page 4; 11 April 1913, page 4, in the *Public Opinion* newspaper.)

[104] "Register's Notices," *Public Opinion,* 3 April 1913, page 6; 28 April 1913, page 6; 2 May 1913, page 6.

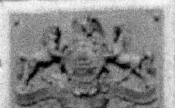

107TH. PENNA. INFANTRY

1ST. BRIG. 2D. DIV.
1ST. CORPS

JULY 1 THE REGIMENT FOUGHT HERE
FROM 1 P.M. UNTIL THE CORPS RETIRED AND
THEN TOOK POSITION ON THE LEFT OF
CEMETERY HILL. IN THE EVENING OF THE
2D MOVED TO THE LEFT TO SUPPORT THE
SECOND CORPS AND AFTER THE REPULSE OF
THE ENEMY RETURNED TO FORMER POSITION
ON THE 3D MOVED SEVERAL TIMES TO BE
IN SOME DIFFERENT PARTS OF THE LINE

```
┌─────────────────────────────────────────┐
│ Thomas KILBORNE (1578-1640)             │
│        & Frances MOODY (1584-1650)      │
└─────────────────────────────────────────┘

┌─────────────────────────────────────────┐
│ John KILBOURN (1624-1703)               │
│        & Sarah BRONSON (?-1711)         │
└─────────────────────────────────────────┘

┌─────────────────────────────────────────┐
│ Abraham KILBURN (1675-1713)             │
│        & Sarah GOODRICH (1679-1719)     │
└─────────────────────────────────────────┘

┌─────────────────────────────────────────┐
│ Abraham KILBOURN (1708-1776)            │
│        & Rebecca DICKINSON (1705-1767)  │
└─────────────────────────────────────────┘

┌───────────────────────────────────────────┐
│ Issac KILBOURN (1737-1807)                │
│      & Mehitable DOOLITTLE (1738-before 1787)│
└───────────────────────────────────────────┘

┌───────────────────────────────────────────┐
│ Abraham KILBOURN (1759-1805)              │
│   & Elizabeth DEMARANVILLE (circa 1772-1829)│
└───────────────────────────────────────────┘

┌─────────────────────────────────────────┐
│ David KILBORN (1788-1854)               │
│       & Lucinda PANGBORN (1789-1881)    │
└─────────────────────────────────────────┘

┌───────────────────────────────────────────┐
│ Truman KILBORN (1809-1895)                │
│      & Clarissa BARNES (1825-circa 1845)  │
│      & Amelia Emaline REYNOLDS (1824-1910)│
└───────────────────────────────────────────┘

┌───────────────────────────────────────────┐
│ Churchill Vaughn KILBORN (1840-1882)      │
│      & Emily Elizabeth ALDRICH (1843-1873)│
│      & Eva C. ENTRICAN (1848-1910)        │
└───────────────────────────────────────────┘
```

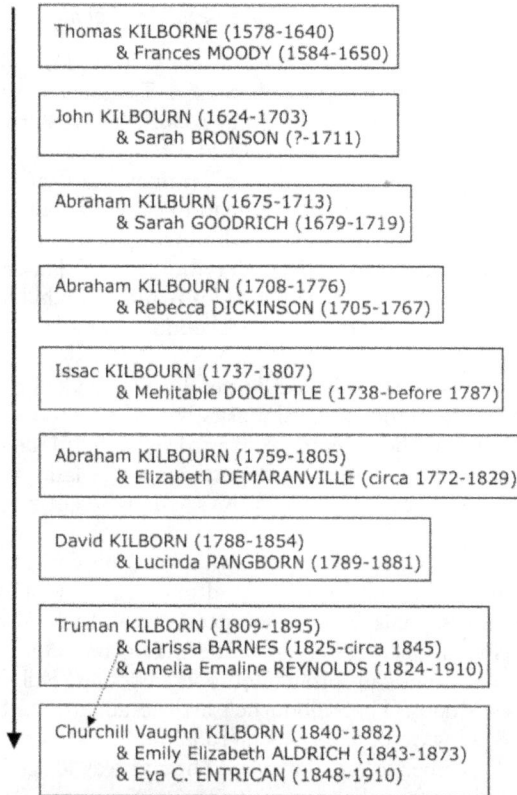

III. The Horsemen of Michigan

CV KILBORN

"Tioga," is the Iroquoian definition of "junction" or "fork." The fork-in-the-road for New England Yankees looking for new timber for the booming shipbuilding industries in Connecticut and Massachusetts was Tioga County, Pennsylvania. By the 1790s, New England was exporting 36 million board feet and 300 ship masts annually.[105] It wasn't going to last and those with foresight saw the need to look for more virgin areas. David Kilbourne, a Vermont lumberjack and his wife Lucinda *nee* Pangborn, pioneered into the Northern Tier of Penn's Woods and built the first sawmill in

---

[105] Defebaugh, James E. *History of The Lumber Industry of America.* Vol. 2. Chicago: American Lumberman, 1907, page 17.

nearby Pike Township, Potter County in 1824.[106] His family, of course, came with him, namely his son, Truman.

Truman first married around 1836, Clarissa Barnes (1825 - died circa 1845), and after her short life, remarried to Amelia Emaline Reynolds, daughter of James. To Truman and Clarissa was born 30 May 1840 in the wild and woodland Pennsylvania County of Potter, Churchill Vaughn Kilborn,[107] who first appears in the 1850 Census in Tioga County,[108] living under the roof of James Reynolds, his step-mother's father. He received his name Churchill from his grandfather Churchill Barnes and his middle name from grandmother Sally Vaughn.

By 1860, Churchill was in nearby Potter County, Pennsylvania, also engaged in the lumber industry.[109]

Going by the copious court records, father Truman had moved to Michigan by 1870,[110] and participated in land speculation. Michigan didn't have the trees "Penn's Woods" enjoyed, so he wheeled-and-dealed in real estate.

"CV," as Churchill was known among his contemporaries, came from a long line of New England and old world ancestors. His alleged earliest male Kilbourne ancestor was Richard Kylborne who lived circa 1395 to 1454 in southern England. But a few centuries later the American progenitor was Thomas Kilborne and wife Frances Moody. The Kilbourne's arrived aboard the Ship *Increase* in the second wave of Pilgrams in 1635, and lived in the Weathersfield area of Connecticut as farmers. Thomas was allegedly killed in an attack arising from a dispute with native Americans, 23 April 1637.

Herein, please refer to the chart at the beginning of the chapter.

---

[106] Thompson, Richard. "Galeton Hit 4213 Population in 1904." Potter County Historical Society. *Historical Sketches of Potter County, Pennsylvania.* Coudersport, Pennsylvania: Journal Press, 1976, page 104.

[107] For our subject the surname has varied over the years out illiteracy or the whim of the Census taker or keeping the name shorter on a tombstone. In the 1850, 1860 Censuses it was KILBORN, In 1870 it was KILBURN, back again in the 1880 Census to KILBORN. From the 15th Century to the present, it has had various spellings: KYLBORN, KILBORNE, KYLBOURN, KILBURNE, KILBORNE but was predominantly KILBOURN. The descendants of Churchill and Emily settled upon KILBOURNE by the early 1900s.

[108] "1850 United States Census," Westfield Township, Tioga County, Pennsylvania. NARA M432; Roll 830; Page 288A; Line 16. Under the James Runnels [sic] family.

[109] "1860 United States Census," Hector Township, Potter County, Pennsylvania. NARA M653; Roll 1177; Page 142.

[110] "1870 United States Census," Deerfield Township, Mecosta County, Michigan. NARA M593; Roll 690; Page 47.

A son of Thomas was John, who married Sarah Bronson. John rose to prominence as a Connecticut State Representative for a number of years.

John's son was Abraham[1], who married Sarah Goodrich. Abraham[1] had a son, also named Abraham [2], a Connecticut public servant for many years and was the first to propose the separation of the colonies from England, but died before the signing of the Declaration of Independence. Apparently, he successfully escaped the King's arrest and the hang-man's noose for his views. He married Rebecca Dickinson, who in Biblical fashion, together named a son Isaac who married Mehitable Doolittle.

Isaac begot son Abraham[3] who fought as a Revolutionary War soldier, enlisting in 1777 as a private in Captain Joseph Allen Wright's company, Colonel Philip Burr Bradley's Connecticut Fifth Regiment. He married Elizabeth DeMaranville, daughter of another Revolutionary soldier, Stephen DeMaranville (1750-1827). Stephen was a spy for George Washington, and served as a Private in Capt. Wilcox's Company, Col. Nathaniel Freeman's Regiment. He enlisted 29 September 1777 for 30 days service on a secret expedition to Rhode Island. Roll sworn to in Suffolk County, Massachusetts[111] and, "[w]as at Saratoga, N.Y., when Burgoyne surrendered and [a] guard over prisoners sent to Boston, Massachusetts."[112]

Abraham[3] and Elizabeth brought forth son, David, previously noted, who, in search of more timber, is first found in 1810 in Essex County, New York. He moved to Tioga County, Pennsylvania, by 1820,[113] and later to Potter County, Pennsylvania, by 1840,[114] establishing prosperous lumbering operations for him and his progeny.

David's son, Truman, previously cited, arrived in Michigan by 1870. First wife, Clarissa, gave him three children, of which one was CV, and Truman's second wife Amelia, gave him eight additional children, making eleven offspring.

Despite a long pedigree of successful ancestors, CV came to Montcalm County, by way of Ionia County, Michigan shortly after

---

[111] Massachusetts Archive: *Massachusetts Soldiers and Sailors of the Revolutionary War*, Volume IV.

[112] Randall, George L. *DeMaranville Genealogy, Descendants of Louis De-Maranville*. New Bedford, Massachusetts, 1921.

[113] "1820 United States Census," Delmar Township, Tioga County, Pennsylvania, page 21.

[114] "1840 United States Census," Hector Township, Potter County, Pennsylvania, page 270.

1860[115] — looking to make his own way. He farmed in Montcalm County and increased his love for horses, inherited from his father Truman, who passed down a red salve recipe for the beasties which remains in the family today. But life on the flat lands of central Michigan was bleak and harsh. It wasn't long before a young CV was enticed by the War engulfing the nation south and east of him.

THE WAR, 1864

In August 1864, the War was in it's third year and it showed no signs of relenting despite the high watermark Battle of Gettysburg in July 1863. General Ulysses S. Grant had assumed the command of Union Army forces in the East and engaged in attrition in Virginia against Lee's Army of Virginia. General William Tecumseh, at the same time, was quickly approaching Atlanta, Georgia with his scorched-earth "March to the Sea." It was evident to the Confederacy they were losing the war but hoping for foreign intervention to save them — but it wasn't forthcoming.

Despite lackluster results on the battlefield the Lincoln Administration was more skillful in the circles of international diplomacy. Lincoln warned other nations, particularly England and France,[116] who were significant importers of cotton[117] before the conflict, that recognition of the Confederacy would lead to a declaration of war. But England's loss of cotton gained in its export of ships, armaments, and processed cotton products (clothes, particularly uniforms) to the Northern states.[118] European nations recognized the geographical distance — an ocean away — and knew intervening into domestic civil wars were quagmires.

Whatever led him, a single man, at age 24, CV volunteered for one year on 22 August 1864 at Grand Rapids credited to Eureka, Montcalm County, Michigan. Described as a farmer having hazel eyes, brown hair, light complexion, and at 5 feet 11 inches tall. Ten days later, he mustered into Company E, 10th Regiment Michigan Volunteer Cavalry, at Jackson, as a private. They paid him a bounty fee of $33.33 for joining.

---

[115] "1860 United States Census," Hector Township, Potter County, Pennsylvania. NARA M653; Roll 1177; Page 142.

[116] France was engaged in a dangerous imperialistic adventure going on in the "Second Franco-Mexican War."

[117] England experienced a 90% drop in Confederate imports. The Port of New York also suffered: a nearly 50% drop in imports in 1859-60. *New York Times*, "Our Civil War and European Trade," 2 October 1861, page 2.

[118] Foreman, Amanda. *A World on Fire: An Epic History of Two Nations Divided*. London: Penguin, 2010.

10th Regiment commander
General Luther Stephen
Trowbridge (1836-1912)
(Library of Congress)

10th Regiment, Company E
commander, Captain Harvey E.
Light (1834-1921)
(Library of Congress)

Before CVs enlistment, the regiment had left for Lexington, Kentucky, post-organization in the summer and fall of 1863, arriving 5 December 1863, staying for a week. They traversed in more pleasant weather to report in Knoxville, Tennessee by February 1864. The company became attached to the 2nd Brigade, 4th Division, 23rd Corps of the Union Army. "To all who participated in it, that march across the mountains will long be remembered as one of especial discomfort."[119]

Sarcastically, his regimental commander, General Trowbridge later wrote: "During the month of March, two companies, under Captain Light, were detached for service at Knoxville. The command was afterwards increased to four companies under the same officer. The service was pleasant and important, consisting of picket duty, courier and escort duty, with some scouting when occasion required. They had the disadvantage, however, of being away from the regiment and missing many of its interesting and exciting experiences."[120]

---

[119] Trowbridge, General L.[uther] S.[tephen]. *A Brief History of the Tenth Michigan Cavalry.* Detroit: Friesema Bros. Printing Co., 1908; page 10.
[120] ibid·, page 12.

Company E, remained behind to garrison Knoxville.[121] A charismatic Greenville nurseryman and former Sheriff of Montcalm County, Michigan, Captain (later Major) Harvey E. Light, commanded Company E.

CV arrived in late August in Knoxville, one of the recruits that "On the 13th [August 1864] Colonel Trowbridge was ordered to Michigan to hurry forward a large number of men who were said to have been enlisted for the regiment, and were awaiting transportation."[122]

The long travel was apparently uneventful until 15 October 1864 when CV was listed as being sick in the Holston General Hospital in Knoxville. The illness unknown, but on 24 October 1864 he was ordered on a 20-day furlough from the hospital, and ordered to report to the Commanding Officer at the Detroit Barracks and the Superintendent of hospitals for examination. The Detroit Barracks, during the War, was primarily an induction center with the small Independent Company, Michigan Volunteer Infantry serving as Provost Guard. Despite its location, the barracks was little used during the War. CVs records never revealed the nature of his illness, but his leave-of-absence turned out to be a 76-day furlough. On 8 January 1865, he voluntarily reported back to his unit in Knoxville.

The muster roll of 9 January 1865, at the Detroit Barracks, listed him in a detachment of "Convalescents & Straggler[s]." Later in January or February, he was listed as absent from his unit but was "On detached service Wash. Col. Hawley." The "Col. Hawley" is believed to be William Hawley, who, during this period, commanded the Second Brigade in the First Division of XX Corps. Under Hawley were the Second Massachusetts, Thirteenth New Jersey, 107th New York, 150th New York, and the Third Wisconsin Infantry regiments. This time period was the Campaign of the Carolinas in continuity with Sherman's March to the Sea campaign. What "detached service" CV was involved, remains a mystery with no records finding CV serving in any other unit.

On 12 June 1865, he was discharged from the service at Knoxville and was paid $100.49 for clothing, a $33.33 bounty fee, $7.96 for transportation while on furlough, and was noted as entitled to subsistence pay during his leave.

CV GOES HOME

"No arrangements for a school were made until the next spring, when Mr. Hunt canvassed the township and found it practicable, the

---

[121] Dyer, Volume II, page 1275.

[122] Trowbridge, page 28.

settlers subscribing one dollar per scholar for the purpose of employ-
ing a teacher. As there were but seven pupils in the district the sum
was not large. Elizabeth Aldrich was engaged to teach, for which the
district agreed to pay one dollar and fifty cents per week, board not
included. The pupils' names were Margaret Aldrich. Phoebe Smith,
Byron Smith, Albert Hunt, Cornelius Mart, Ida Whitmore and
Agnes Whitmore. Miss Aldrich, at the time she taught this school,
was sixteen years of age. She taught, three months, the parents in
the district making up by subscription the necessary fund. She was
also employed to teach the next school year, wages being increased to
two dollars and fifty cents per week. She subsequently became the
wife of C. V. Kilborn."[123]

It was this June, 1865 when CV returned home, and he promptly married that school teacher Emily Elizabeth ("Libby") Aldrich
(1843-1873), daughter of Harris Aldrich (1809-died after 1852) and
of Rebecca Stuart (1820-1889).

The Kilborn's begot children:
i.   Clarisa Sophonia (1866-1945); who married Dr. Webster Clark
     Martin
ii. Thomas Oscar (1868-1934); married Amelia Hannah Elizabeth
     Pickles
iii. Agnes Elizabeth (1870-1929); married Horatio W. "Ray" Whitsell
iv. Asa Truman (1873-1928); married Gertrude "Maude" Stingle.
     Libby died from childbirth from the last child Asa, just short of her
     thirtieth birthday.

CV served as a Town Clerk for Douglass Township from
1867-68 and again in 1874-75.

CV remarried 5 February 1874 to Eva C. Entrican (1848-1910),
daughter of William W. Entrican, who was the first person to be
buried in the first public cemetery in Douglass Township on the
Aldrich farm.[124] Eva also had two brothers who served in the Civil
War: George W. and Albert L. Entrican, both of whom joined Company K, 21st Regiment Michigan Infantry in August of 1862. Brother Albert was severely wounded in the War, but survived it. The

---

[123] Dasef, John W. *History of Montcalm County, Michigan; Its People, Industries and Institutions.* Indianapolis, Indiana: B.F. Bowen & Company Inc.,
1916; Volume 2, page 305. Also see: Schenck, John S. *The History of Ionia &
Montcalm Counties, Michigan.* Philadelphia: D. W. Ensign & Co., 1881, page 442.
[124] Dasef, Volume 1, page 129.

```
        ┌─────────────────────────────────┐
        │         Asahel ALDRICH          │
        │               &                 │
        │  Elizabeth Lucinda BIRDSALL     │
        └─────────────────────────────────┘

┌──────────────────┐  ┌──────────────────┐  ┌──────────────────┐
│  Harris ALDRICH  │──│ Rebecca STUART   │──│ Stephen ALDRICH  │
└──────────────────┘  └──────────────────┘  └──────────────────┘

        ┌──────────────────┐  ┌──────────────────────────────┐
        │ Emma Elizabeth   │──│ Churchill Vaughn "CV" KILBORN │
        │ "Libby" ALDRICH  │  │                              │
        └──────────────────┘  └──────────────────────────────┘
```

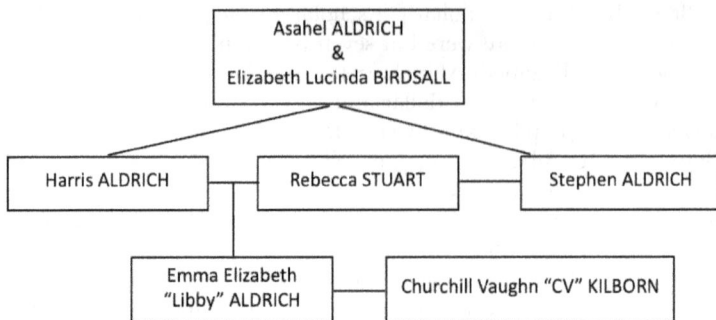

hamlet Entrican was named after George in honor of being first to enlist in the Union Army.[125] CV and Eva's union begot:

v. Musey Ethel (1876-1912); who married Joseph R. Hunt
vi. Elmer Lewellyn (1881-1928); married Grace M. Parks.

Family lore suggests CV and Eva had an unhappy marriage, leading to speculation about his death:

"C.V. Kilbourn of Douglas Township met with a serious, and perhaps fatal accident Monday. He and his … [step-brother John Moranville Kilbourne] were examining their revolver, for what purpose we did not learn, and the first thing his brother knew C.V's revolver went off and inspection showed that the ball had taken effect near the center of the forehead. The physician that was called reports that the injury will probably be fatal."[126]

CV lingered for about a week and life ended at a short 42 years of age, 6 September 1882.

Eva continued on with her life. She filed a pension application in 1890, but the outcome is not found. She passed away in Missaukee County, Michigan at 61 years of age in 1910.

HARRIS & STEPHEN ALDRICH

Families can be complicated social units. The romanticized Nineteenth Century of stability and "a simpler life" can be found in much contemporary popular literature. But the truth be told, life in the pioneering days of America were fraught with discord, deaths, and their own dramas.

---

[125] Ronig, Walter. *Michigan Place Names. Grosse Pointe, Michigan: 1973.* Re-published by Great Lakes Books, Waynes University Press, Detroit, 1986, page 185.

[126] *Stanton Weekly Clipper,* newspaper, Stanton, Montcalm County, Michigan. 8 September 1882, page 1, column 2. Courtesy, Elizabeth Clare Martin Johnson.

CV's young wife, Libby Aldrich, was not excused from the tumult of family life in the rural and harsh Michigan habitat.

Her father, Harris Aldrich, a somewhat mysterious character, is important in learning the family dynamics.

HARRIS ALDRICH

Harris was born on 17 October 1809 in Palmyra, Wayne County, New York, the seventh generation from an ancient New England family, established by George Aldrich and his wife, Katherine *nee* Seald. They came to America from England in November 1631, probably on the ship *Lyon*, first settling in Dorchester, Massachusetts. A few generations later, their progeny aligned themselves with the Society of Friends (Quakers). It was Harris's father, Asahel, and mother Elizabeth Lucinda Birdsall, that migrated from Massachusetts to Connecticut, then to the Rochester, New York area, and later to Michigan. In 1834, Asahel, Elizabeth, and births of their children were recorded at the Farmington Monthly Meeting.[127]

Since 1816, the Farmington Monthly Meeting was a hub of progressive ideals, promoting emancipations of African-Americans, women, Native Americans, and pacifism. Harris and his kin left the area before Lucretia Mott, Elizabeth Cady Stanton, and Susan B. Anthony each spoke at the Meeting.

The Meeting later supported the 1848 pivotal Seneca Falls convention.

"The first pastor of the Adrian Friends Meetinghouse (1835-1841) was Daniel Smith, whose famous Quaker abolitionist daughter Laura Smith Haviland (1808-1898) is interred in the church cemetery. The congregation was part of the New York Yearly Meeting until 1869 and then became part of the Ohio Yearly Meeting. Friends worshipped in this building for the first time on June 11, 1835."[128]

Laura Smith Haviland (1808-1898). *From her book A Woman's Life Work: Labors and Experiences, 1882.*

In May 1839, Harris purchased 40

---

[127] Frost, Josephine C.; Friends, Society of. Quaker Records From Farmington Monthly Meeting, Ontario County, New York. Library of Congress, 1910.

[128] Brennan, John. *The Michigan Historical Marker Web Site.* www.michmarkers.com/default?page=L1844. January 2020.

acres of land in Michigan,[129] bringing him back to Branch County, Michigan, by 1840,[130] and two years later marriage to Rebecca Stuart.[131]

Because of his marriage to Presbyterian outsider, Rebecca, a year later, Harris was discharged from the Adrian Quakers Meeting for having a "marriage out of unity" and was "disowned."[132]

Undaunted, Harris and Rebecca farmed the land and led their lives as other folks, and begot Libby and her brother Thomas Stuart Aldrich in 1845.[133]

THE DISAPPEARANCE OF HARRIS

In May, 1852, an unknown seismic event in the young family's fortunes occurred, when the Sheriff put Harris's farm up for sale:

"By virtue of an execution issued out of the Branch County Court against the Goods, Chattels, Lands and Tenements of Harris Aldrich, I have levied upon the following Lands to wit: The east half of the north west quarter of section 'No. 31' Town five south of Range No. Six west, in Branch County, the property of Harris Aldrich; which I shall sell at public vendue [sic] at the Court House in the village of Coldwater, on the 22d day of May 1852, at 2 o'clock P.M. March 29, 1852 PHILO PORTER, Sheriff."[134]

All records of Harris seem to disappear after 1852 and he was often confused with another Harris Aldrich in a nearby county. Despite decades of research and folklore, and recent intense search by Elisabeth Clare Martin Johnson and by this author, nothing can be found of any "Harris Aldrich" roughly matching his known profile after 1852. He either died or left the area — often confused with another discounted and unrelated Harris Aldrich who settled in Iowa.

Harris and Rebecca had two children:

i.   Libby (above, married to Churchill Vaughn Kilborn), and

---

[129] Michigan, Homestead and Cash Entry Patents, Pre-1908. Issue Date of 1 May 1839; statutory reference 3 Stat. 566; sale-cash entry.

[130] "1840 United States Census," Girard Township, Branch County, Michigan. NARA M704; Roll 203; Page 104.

[131] *Coldwater Sentinel,* newspaper, Coldwater, Branch County, Michigan. "Married. In Bronson, on Monday, the 2d inst. by Emerson March, Esq., Mr. Harris Aldrich, of Girard, Miss Rebecca Stuart, both of this county." 13 May 1842 (Courtesy of Elisabeth Clare Martin Johnson)

[132] *Friends, Society of. U. S. Encyclopedia of American Quaker Genealogy. Volumes I - IV, 1607-1943.* Library of Congress, 1910. Volume IV, page 1349.

[133] "1850 United States Census," Girard Township, Branch County, Michigan. NARA M432; Roll 347; Page 308A; Family 176.

[134] *Coldwater Sentinel,* 21 May 1852, page 4.

ii. Thomas Stuart (1845-1862).

Libby's mother, Rebecca Stuart Aldrich, was not unfaltering by any plight that came her way. Born in Ireland but of Scots heritage as suggested by her surname,[135] and reported on the 1870 census.[136] She, her parents, Thomas Stuart and Margery *nee* McBride, and siblings were immigrants to America from "Carlay," Ireland,[137] settling in New York State by the mid-1820s and, eventually to Michigan by the 1840s. She became accustomed to the hard life on the fringes of the Euro-centric America frontier.

STEPHEN ALDRICH

Not to be abandoned, Rebecca married Harris's 10-year-younger brother, Stephen Aldrich (1819-1891) on 31 August 1853,[138] in Marshall, Calhoun County, Michigan. Therefore, becoming the step-father of Libby and the future guiding hand of the family.

The Stephen and Rebecca union begot:

iii. Agnes Margarie (1854-1927), who married Oscar Mortimer Kilborn (1852-1924), a distant cousin of CV

iv. Margaret Frances (1857-1931); married John N. Clement (1859-1941), a Canadian immigrant.

---

[135] Dasef, Volume 2, page 519. Also, her Census records, although conflicting at times, are consistent with her origins and time frames. The surname "Stuart" or "Stewart" were used.

[136] Place of Birth: "Scotland"; 1870 US Census, Douglass Township, Montcalm County, Michigan; Page 4; Dwelling 39; Family 39; Line 38. The 1850 and 1860 censuses say she was born in New York state; the 1880 census says born in Ireland. We can only guess which reports are from her or the whims of a passing-by census taker.

[137] According to the family Bible reported by Vicki Cox. Note: no "Carlay" could be found in gazetteers, but that doesn't mean it didn't exist. Perhaps the town was lost to clearances or abandonment.

[138] Marriage certificate; married by Joseph Frank, Justice-of-the-Peace. "Stephen Aldrich and Rebecca Aldrich

    State of Michigan | Calhoun Co.

This certifies that on the 31st day of August A.D. 1853 at Marshall in the Co. of Calhoun aforesaid I Joined in Matrimony Stephen Aldrich of Girard [illegible] the State of Michigan aged 31 years and Rebecca Aldrich of Girard in the State of Michigan aged 30 years. (signed) Joseph [illegible] Frank, Justice of the Peace. In the presence of Jane L. Johnston of Marshall Norris J. Frank of Marshall

    Recorded Aug 31, 1853"

Rebecca and Stephen's union was steady. Before his marriage to Rebecca, Stephen, always single, lived with his mother, sister Desire, and brother Amos in 1850.[139]

"Stephen Aldrich, father of Mrs. Margaret Aldrich) Clement, was born in Connecticut. When a young men he went to New York and located near Rochester, later moving to Coldwater, Michigan, where he was married to Rebecca Stewart. Rebecca Stewart was born in Ireland, of Scotch parentage, and was four years old when her family came to this country and located first in New York state and later moved to Michigan. Rebecca Stewart was first married to Harris Aldrich, a brother of Stephen, and to this marriage were born two children, Elizabeth and Thomas. Stephen Aldrich and Rebecca Stewart were married in 1854 and came to Montcalm county, settling in what is now Douglass township, the name of which was selected by Mrs. Rebecca Aldrich. Mr. and Mrs. Stephen Aldrich were the parents of two children, Agnes and Margaret. Agnes Aldrich married Oscar Kilborn and lives in Sacramento, California. During the Civil War Stephen Aldrich enlisted in the Union army in September, 1862, and served three years. He was a well-known farmer of this county. Mrs. Aldrich was a member of the Methodist church."[140]

"James Farnsworth pre-empted eighty acres on the east half of section 9, but within a year he sold to Stephen Aldrich, who in the summer of 1854 came into the town-ship to look for government land. His wife, formerly Miss Rebecca Stewart, whose parents settled in the township of Gilead, now the township of Noble, Branch Co., and became permanent settlers there with the family, came to the township of Douglass in the fall of 1854. They still reside on the farm purchased at this time, and are the only couple now living in the township who settled here in that year.

Mr. Aldrich went to work immediately to clear and improve his farm. The following spring he set out the first fruit-trees in Douglass."[141]

Life was hard on those spare Michigan lands.

"The year 1857 was one of hunger and need. Late frosts had completely destroyed the fields of corn and other crops. Even wild game became scarce. Peter Johnson left his wife and two small children, an infant girls and Olive of two and on-half years, to find work in Greenville. During his absence Mrs. Johnson became ill and was cared for by Mrs. Rebecca Aldrich who walked daily on the rough

---

[139] "1850 United States Census," Girard Township, Branch County, Michigan. NARA M432; Roll 347; Page 305A; Family 128.

[140] Dasef, Volume 2, page 519.

[141] Dasef, Volume I, pages 126-127.

wagon road through the trees. When Mrs. Johnson recovery Mrs. Aldrich fell sick and it may have been Stephen Aldrich who himself came to ask her to help Rebecca and two small girls, Margaret age five and Agnes age 3. Mrs. Johnson, leaving her own two children for a short time, hurried over to Mrs. Goodwater's to ask her to stay with her little ones. On their return to the Johnson cabin they were horrified to find it engulfed in flames and the roof about to fall in."[142]

"In the 1860's a school and cemetery had been established a half mile north on the farm of Stephen Aldrich on what is now Nevins road."[143]

"The burying ground for the white settlers of Douglass township was set aside by Stephen Aldrich on his farm at the time of the death of his nephew and foster [step] son Thomas Aldrich who died at the age of 17, April 16, 1862. Stephen had married his brother's widow Rebecca and Tom seemed the same as his own son."[144]

Stephen was a civic man. In 1857, the township of Cato, Montcalm County became a new governmental entity and Stephen was elected Justice-of-the-Peace and District Number 2 overseer.[145] And in 1862, he became Treasurer of Pine Township.[146] In a re-organization, part of Cato became Pine Township in 1862. Stephen was elected Treasurer.[147] But the looming Civil War pulled him away from family, farm, and local duties.

STEPHEN GOES TO WAR.

By the time of Stephen's enlistment, 13 September 1862, in Greenville, Montcalm County, Michigan as a "Three-Year Man," into Company D, 7th Michigan Cavalry Regiment, the war for the Union was about to take a turn for the worse. A few days before Stephen's enlistment, McClellan was pursuing Lee northward during the 4-9th. They eventually engaged with each other at Sharpsburg, Maryland (also known as "Antietam") on the 17th. The Battle of Antietam, the most bloodied clash to date, essentially was a draw: McClellan stopped Lee's invasion of the North but extracted a high cost from the Union forces.

---

142 Gustafson, A. M. *Douglass, A Michigan Township.* 1982, page 4. Story by Alger Johnson.

143 Ibid., Page 187.

144 Schneck, Page 484.

145 Ibid., page 438.

146 Gustafson, page 3.

147 Schenck, page 484.

7th Michigan Cavalry, Company D commander, Captain George Armstrong Armstrong Custer (1839-1876). *(Library of Congress)*

Stephen, mustered-in on 13 November 1862, at Grand Rapids, Michigan. Traveling to the Washington, D.C. area as part of the defenses of Washington, assigned to 22 Corps, Second Brigade, Third Division[148] by January-February 1863, he was present for those muster calls.

Unfortunately, from March to August 1863, he was absent from his post due to an unknown illness at Columbian Hospital, Washington, D.C.[149] Thus, he missed the Battle of Gettysburg in July and the actions that propelled Company D's commander and then little known social climber George Armstrong Custer into history. Custer is better known for the military catastrophe and his death at "The Last Stand" at Little Bighorn in 1876. Nevertheless, Custer's skillful actions at Gettysburg earned him a good reputation.

Despite his illness, Private Aldrich was able to sign a petition to erect the township of Douglass in February 1864 — previously part of Pine township. "The naming of this township seems to have cause the greatest difficulty." As the name came from and was in honor of Stephen A. Douglas, a presidential rival of Abraham Lincoln.[150]

Stephen reported present for his unit, September and October 1863 and participated in reconnaissance in Virginia.[151]

Alas, from November 1863 to October 1864, he again became ill to an unknown sickness and was in hospital "1637"[152] in the Washington, D.C. area. But in November and part of December muster, he was moved to Philadelphia, then Pittsburgh, then to Iowa for reasons unknown. From 31 December 1864 to 30 April 1865, he was absent from his regular unit, but at Remount Camp, Pleasant Valley, Maryland. The Camp was part of the Quartermaster Corps

---

[148] Dyer, page 1273.

[149] Now Columbian College, on Meridan Hill, west of 14th Street Road, later to become part of the George Washington University system in 1904.

[150] Dasef. Volume I, page 124.

[151] Dyer, Volume II, page 1273.

[152] Unknown name.

that provided horses and training to its soldiers, and a bivouac of repose after battle or extended illness. From May to 31 August 1865, he was absent but on detached service at Ft. Leavenworth, Kansas, and on 15 December 1865, per General Order 77, War Department 65,[153] he was mustered out of military service.

After the War, Stephen returned to his duties at home. He appears in the 1870[154] and 1880[155] Census records, quietly farming the land.

Starting in 1888, Quit Claims to Rebecca's share (Oscar Kilbourne, Administrator) of Elizabeth Aldrich Kilbourne's children and husband to Agnes Aldrich, were made. On 23 June 1888, Rebecca deeded the 40 acres to daughter Margaret and Agnes, postmortem recorded 28 December 1889.

THE CLOSING OF LIFE

Wife Rebecca passed away in August 1889, age 68. Family lore says the later years of her life were spent in bed or a chair after falling off a horse.[156]

In 1890, like many veterans of the War, Stephen became a member of the G.A.R. Post 81 "Osmer F. Cole," along with CV Kilborn.[157] And, he is found in the special 1890 Census of Civil War veterans.[158]

Stephen would strike the tent 21 August 1891 in the township he loved, age 71 years.[159]

---

[153] General Order Number 77, 6 June 1863, Richmond, Virginia by S. Cooper, Adjutant and Inspector General. "When an infantry soldier is detailed as a courier, under paragraph III, General Orders, No. 7, current series, and shall keep himself provided with a serviceable horse, he will be allowed forty cents per day for the use and risk of his horse."

[154] "1870 United States Census," Douglass Township, Montcalm County, Michigan. NARA M593; Roll 692; Page 65B; Family 39.

[155] "1880 United States Census," Douglass Township, Montcalm County, Michigan. Roll 596; Sheet 3A; Enumeration District 226.

[156] Doyle, Vena Emily Kilbourne. Letter, 22 April 1981.

[157] Gustafson. Page 55.

[158] "1890 US Special Census Schedule. — Surviving Soldiers, Sailors, and Marines, and Widows, etc." [of the Civil War] NARA M123, Montcalm County, Michigan; Line 34.

[159] Death record number 574.

IV. Neighbors and Kin

IV. Neighbors and Kin.

Amonth after the Battle of Antietam, on 11 October 1862, Confederate General J.E.B. Stuart's cavalrymen rode into Fairfield after a horse raid into Mercersburg, Pennsylvania the day before. They robbed a few stores and kidnapped a couple of citizens as civilian prisoners-of-war on their way out of Gettysburg.

A few months later, gray-clothed uniforms trampled the bustling farms and neighbors in June and July 1863, but the these soldiers were not strangers to the area. The Shulley farm was just under two miles south of the hamlet of Fairfield and some ten miles from the Mason-Dixon Line, endured the intrusions.

THE BATTLE OF FAIRFIELD

Nevertheless, again, in June 1863, the Army of Northern Virginia attempted to invade the North after a tactical draw between the combatants at Antietam, making their way up into the Pennsylvania Franklin and Adams counties. On 21 June, the 14th Virginia Cavalry raided near Fairfield but were repulsed by First Troop, Philadelphia City Cavalry. A week later, 28 June, soldiers from Crenshaw's Virginia Battery relieved the local citizens in Carroll's Valley of their horses. Shots were fired at a small skirmish at Fountain Dale, capturing some fleeing Confederates. But the next day the 24th Regiment, North Carolina, and 42nd Regiment, Mississippi, pushed forward and encamped around Fairfield. A skirmish ensued, and the rebels rode away. On 30 June, elements of the 8th Illinois Cavalry stumbled upon rebel skirmishers near Jack's Mountain near Peter Musselman's farm, near Tom's Creek, but there were no casualties.[160]

A day later these events were overshadowed by the events just to the east of the town, and south of Gettysburg, the most massive land-mass battle in North America, 1-3 July 1863, absorbed the attention — Gettysburg.

As the Confederate forces trickled out in retreat, a little known "Battle of Fairfield" transpired with a cavalry engagement on 3 July. It was the outnumbered 2,000 men of the Union's 6th U.S. Cavalry, Wesley Merritt's Brigade, versus Grumble Jones' Brigade superior force of Stuart's Cavalry.

The 6th U.S. Cavalry, having discovered Confederate wagon trains rolling out of Fairfield, met the 7th Virginia Cavalry, engaged, pushing them off the ridge with disastrous results. The federal troops lost nearly half its force, with six killed, twenty-eight wounded, and 208 missing and presumed captured soldiers. The Confederate 6th

[160] Thomas, Sarah Sites; Smith, Tim; Kross, Gary; Thomas, Dean S. *Fairfield in the Civil War.* Gettysburg, Pennsylvania: 2011: Thomas Publications; for the Fairfield Sesquicentennial Committee. Pages 31, 39-40, 42.

and 7th Cavalry lost eleven killed, thirty-nine wounded, and seven missing in action.[161] A driving rainstorm in the afternoon of the 4th of July prevented the 6th U.S. from pursuing, and the rebels escaped under its cover. The Confederate victory secured the Hagerstown Road, allowing parts of the Army of Northern Virginia to escape. After the fighting ended, the Fairfield town folks cared for many wounded soldiers on both sides. When Union forces finally arrived on 5 July, they "...found 871 wounded soldiers under the care of Confederate doctors B.F. Ward of the 11th Mississippi and William Randolph Wilson of the 1st Virginia Cavalry."[162]

By 5 July, the Confederate retreat was in full swing. Union forces marched into Fairfield the next day and drove down Iron Springs Road, finding rebels near the Maria iron furnace, owned by Thaddeus Stevens. Fighting ensued with casualties brought upon the North Carolinians.[163] Within a few days, Confederate forces were out of the area.

At age 26, Fred Shulley[164] was too busy helping his father operate a large, well-established farmstead in Hamiltonban Township, just southwest of Gettysburg. Many of his neighbors and kin weren't around, having enlisted into the nine-months service of the 165th Pennsylvania Infantry Regiment "Drafted Militia" or into the 26th Emergency Militia a few months before the infamous Battle that purloined the county seat's name and its civilian resources into the history books.

The Company C soldiers of the 165th, overwhelmingly from Adams County were, ironically, away in Virginia during the unfortunate battleground that landed on their farms.[165] Present for battle, but unprepared, the green 26th, composed of local students, adventurers, farmers, some without uniforms, declaring every man for himself, skedaddled away after the first hours clash heading northeast to the state Capitol, Harrisburg, or taken prisoner-of-war.[166] We can only guess that the Shulley family temporarily left the farm or successfully hid from the Confederate rebels pillaging the surrounding area.

---

[161] Ibid., et al. page 61.

[162] Ibid., et al. page 58.

[163] Ibid., et al. page 46.

[164] Herein "FredM" for brevity.

[165] Bates, Volume IV, pages 1084-1085.

[166] Petruzzi, J. David and Stanley, Steven. "They Came with Barbarian Yells and Smoking Pistols" *American Battlefield Trust*, https://www.battlefields.org/learn/articles/they-came-barbarian-yells-and-smoking-pistols

```
        ┌─────────────────────┐     ┌─────────────────────┐
        │  Frederick SHULLEY  │─M─│  Mary Leah ?REIFF?   │
        │      1748-1841      │     │      1753-1832       │
        └─────────────────────┘     └─────────────────────┘

┌──────────────┐   ┌──────────────────────┐
│ David REIFF II│─M─│ Elizabeth Mary SHULLEY│
│    1783-?     │   │      1775-1854        │
└──────────────┘   └──────────────────────┘

   ┌──────────────────────┐          ┌─────────────────────┐
   │ Mary Elizabeth REIFF  │────M────│  Frederick SHULLEY  │
   │      1811-1895        │          │     1784-1869       │
   └──────────────────────┘          └─────────────────────┘
```

© 2020 Curt Sanders. All Rights Reserved.

```
        ┌──────────────────────┐     ┌─────────────────────────┐
        │ Frederick M. SHULLEY │─M─│ Lucretia Virginia RILEY  │
        │      1837-1911       │     │       1844-1922          │
        └──────────────────────┘     └─────────────────────────┘
```

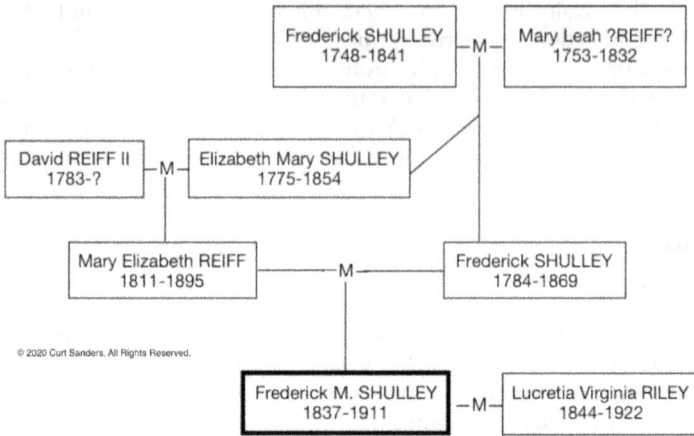

Previously, on 27 November 1862, FredM wedded, at the bride's home in nearby Liberty Township, to Lucretia Virginia Riley, daughter of Barnabas Riley and Mary *nee* Sheets.[167] Lucretia's brother-in-law, the Lutheran Rev. William Gerhardt (married to her sister Lucinda Adeline Riley), performed the ceremony.[168]

Despite strengthened Draft powers in early March 1863, the local Provost Marshall, unknowingly overlooked FredM's potential military service.[169] Perhaps the draft oversight was because his father, Fred Sr.[170] was a well-to-do farmer in the county, and his father-in-law Barnabas had ties to the Republican Party — especially to the local Congressman Thaddeus Stevens — his employer. But by June 1863, he was within the pressure of the local draft board and presented his lawful registration.[171]

The early Shulley's blended into the south-central Pennsylvania community dominated by German speaking and Scot-Irish denizens. Going by family anecdotes, the Shulley's had Swiss-Germanic ori-

---

[167] "Out of the Past," *Gettysburg Times,* Gettysburg, Adams County, Pennsylvania, newspaper, 13 December 1937, page 4. Also, attested to in his Pension Claims.

[168] "Out of the Past," *Gettysburg Times*, 13 December 1937, page 4.

[169] The Enrollment Act, 12 Stat. 731, enacted 3 March 1863. The act required the enrollment of every male citizen and those immigrants who had filed for citizenship between ages 20-45.

[170] "Fred(2)" for simplicity hereinafter.

[171] Hamiltonban Township, Adams County, Pennsylvania, 16th Congressional District, page 119; age 26, white, farmer, married, born in Pennsylvania.

gins, distinct from their neighbors who were generally from the Palatinate of what is now western Germany. Indeed, in 2018, the author's autosomal DNA (a test from both paternal and maternal genes combined) suggested a "Highly Likely Match" probability from French-speaking Canton Lucerne, in the center of Switzerland, and Canton Grisons, the eastern German speaking populace of Switzerland.[172] Knowing the authors' maternal side probably didn't hale from that region, and the process of elimination of other paternal origins, it is assumed these roots very tentatively confirm the Shulley legend.

An etymological study of the surname Shulley suggests the moniker came out of the 1066 Norman Conquest of England, from France.[173] However, this explanation may be confused with the common mix-up of "Shulley" versus "Shelley" and variations that have dogged researchers in separating the two names.

FREDERICK THE FIRST

FredM's grandfather, also named Frederick, appears as "Frederick Sholly" in 1786.[174] "Sholly" is an Americanized spelling of the old German word "Scholle"[175] loosely meaning "plaice," a flatfish found in shallow water. Frederick the First was allegedly born in 1748 by a family anecdote[176] in Switzerland and died 22 May 1841, most likely on his farm. His extrapolated arrival to Pennsylvania was between 1775-1790. Today, the information is based on what we know from their children:

i. Elizabeth Mary (1775-1854) who married David Reiff, II, and later David Sheets (1775-1854).
ii. Christian (circa 1780-1858).
iii. Frederick Jr. (1784-1869); see below; married Mary Elizabeth "Polly" Reiff (1811-1895).
iv. Susannah (1790-1875) who married Rudolph Saurbaugh.
v. Jacob.
vi. Eva (died before 1841) married to Jacob Freet, Sr.

---

172 www.23andme.com

173 Lowe, Mark Anthony. *Patronymica Britannica, A Dictionary of Family Names of the United Kingdom.* London: John Russel Smith, 1860; page 311 "SHELLEY."

174 "1786 Pennsylvania Septennial Census," Washington Township, Franklin County, Pennsylvania.

175 *Dictionary of American Family Names.* Oxford University Press, 2003.

176 The late family researcher, Maysie Naomi Sanders Riley first put forth this hypothesis from her research in the 1980's.

The surname mildly changed over the years:
- Found in the 1790 Census, he was "Frederick Shelley"[177]
- In the two 1800 Censuses, he was "Frederick Shully" and "Sholly"[178]
- In the 1801 County Tax Assessment, he was "Fred. Shulley."[179]
  - Again "Sholly" in 1810.[180]
  - 1820 "Shally"[181]
  - 1830 "Fredrick Sully Senior"[182]
  - 1840 is was back to "Frederick Sholly"[183]
  - His 1841 Last Will and Testament; "Shully"[184]
- He was laid-to-rest in 1841 in the Lower Marsh Creek Presbyterian Cemetery south of Gettysburg as "Frederick Shulley, Sr."[185] The tombstone cemented the surname for later generations.

Frederick the First's wife was Mary Leah, and her maiden name believed to be Rife or Reif. With her husband, she rests in the Lower Marsh Creek Cemetery, with the tombstone etching 1753-1832.[186] Scant more information is available about her at the time of this narrative.

FREDERICK THE SECOND

The son of Frederick the First, also named Frederick, was born 9 July 1784, presumedly on the family farm. He was the eldest son but fourth in the birth order of seven children. Frederick(2) struck off from his father by 1810 and farmed in nearby Menallen Township,

---

[177] NARA, "1790 US Census, Franklin County, Pennsylvania,: M637.

[178] NARA, "1800 Pennsylvania Septennial Census," Hamiltonban Township, Adams County, Pennsylvania; and the federal Census M32; Page 463.

[179] *1886 History of Adams County, Pennsylvania.* (Originally published as *History of Cumberland and Adams Counties*). Chicago: Warner, Beers & Co., 1886 (reprinted, The Bookmark, Knightstown, Indiana, 1977). Page 303.

[180] NARA, "1810 United States Census," Hamiltonban Township, Adams County, Pennsylvania; M32; Roll 35; Page 463.

[181] NARA, "1820 United States Census," Liberty Township, Adams County, Pennsylvania. M33; Roll 96; page 14.

[182] NARA, "1830 United States Census," Liberty Township, Adams County, Pennsylvania, M19; Roll 143; Page 19.

[183] NARA, "1840 United States Census," Freedom Township, Adams County, Pennsylvania; M704; Roll 435; Page 136.

[184] Will, Adams County, Pennsylvania, Volume C-E, Page 514 number 2215.

[185] www.findagrave.com/memorial/21989158

[186] www.findagrave.com/memorial/77854848

recorded as "Frederick Shuley."[187] Like his father, the surname varied at times, but, remarkably, didn't stray into the "Shelley" spelling. The Census-takers were apparently sensitive to the Shulley's requests.

Fred(2) joined in marriage to Mary Elizabeth *nee* Reiff (1811-1895)[188] on 16 October 1827.[189] Often questioned because of the age differences, a young Pennsylvania Dutch fräulein of 16, and him 43 — but not an unlikely scenario looking at the slowness-to-marry Shulley men. She, too, was also his first cousin, but not unlikely for the close-knit family and within the cultural context of the era.

The life of Fred(2) was mostly uneventful. He worked the family farm, making it a successful enterprise over the years. Fred(2) in the U.S. Census reports:

1810: "Frederick Shuley"[190]
1820: "Fredrick Shally"[191]
1830: "Fredrick Sully Junior"[192]
1840: "Frederick Sholly"[193]
1850: "Fredk. Sholley"[194]
1860: "Frederic Shulley"[195]

Fred(2) died 22 December 1869 presumedly on the family farm and leaving a Last Will,[196] and finally recorded in the Federal Mortality Schedule of 1870 as "Shulley."[197]

---

[187] NARA, "1810 United State Census," Menallen Township, Adams County, Pennsylvania. M252; Roll 44; Page 58.

[188] Tombstone and www.findagrave.com/memorial/17983836

[189] *Gettysburg Complier,* 19 December 1827, page 4. Also in the *Adams Sentinel,* 12 December 1827, page 3 noted as the administrators of her father, David Rife's estate together. He was "Frederick Sholly" and she used her middle name Elizabeth.

[190] 1810, NARA, Menallen Township, Adams County, Pennsylvania; M252; Roll 44; Page 58.

[191] 1820, NARA, Liberty Township, Adams County, Pennsylvania; M33; Roll 96.

[192] 1830, NARA, Ibid.; M19; Roll 143; Page 19.

[193] 1840, NARA, Hamiltonban Township, Adams County, Pennsylvania; M704; Roll 435; Page 33.

[194] 1850, NARA, Ibid.; M432; Roll 743; Line 3-9; Page 148A.

[195] 1860, NARA, Ibid.; M653; Roll 1057; Sheet 7; Line 5-10; Page 249.

[196] Adams County, Pennsylvania Will Book D, page 514.

[197] Federal Mortality Schedule; Adams County, Pennsylvania, page 1.

Fred(2)'s wife, Maria or, "Polly," was taken seriously ill in early May 1895[198] and passed away 29 May 1895.[199]

Fred(2) and Maria raised seven children together:

i.   Sarah S. (c1828-before 1880); married Zephaniah Herbert Carlley
ii. Katherine Ann (1830-1910); married Hiram David Eshelman
iii. Maria Hester (1832-1915); married John C. Shertzer, another veteran of the 209th, later described in this book.
iv. **Frederick M.** (1837-1911); below and later described in this book.
v.   David Christian (1840-1924); married Ruth Lydia Jane Brown
vi. Elizabeth Euphemia (1850-1934); married Oscar F. Sprenkle
vii. John Andrew (1852-1910); married Alice Jane Ramp.

FREDERICK M. THE THIRD

The third generation of "Frederick" was born Frederick M. Shulley, 21 February 1837, in Adams County, Pennsylvania. As previously noted before, herein simplified as "FredM" Shulley.

Regardless of seeing the destruction of Republican Party co-founder and Congressman Thaddeus Steven's Caledonia Iron Works to the west of the county, FredM remained out of the war. Stevens, a never shy harsh critic of the Confederates and the prosecution of the fight against them, he was primarily targeted when the enemy troops came to south-central Pennsylvania.

"A self-contained village, the Caledonia iron works included a large charcoal furnace, rolling mill and associated buildings, stables, storehouses, a company store, and cottages for its 200 workers and their families. Confederate horsemen from Albert Jenkins' brigade had visited the furnace on June 16. In return for the impressment of forty horses and mules belonging to the works, the Rebels had not burned the furnace."[200]

FredM's father-in-law, Barnabas Riley, was a carpenter with the crew who built the Maria Furnace and Steven's Caledonia Iron Works.[201] Ruin came on 26 June 1863, against commander Robert E. Lee's orders, when the 17th Virginia Cavalry left Riley and other workers without an income by burning down the enterprise.

Despite the devastation and pilfering by the Confederate soldiers in 1863, FredM never joined the army until a year later at the burn-

---

[198] Ibid., 4 May 1895, page 1.

[199] Ibid., 8 June 1895, page 4. And *Gettysburg Star & Sentinel*, 11 June 1895, page 3. Also, her tombstone.

[200] explorepahistory.com/hmarker.php?markerId=1-A-1DE

[201] 1886 *History of Adams County...* page 446.

---

ng.. The Iron Furnace of Thad. Stevens, at Caledonia, Franklin county, was completely ruined by the rebels. What they could not burn they destroyed in other ways. Mr. Stephens' loss is estimated at $100,000.

Wayne County Herald, Honesdale, Pennsylvania, 16 July 1863, page 1.

ing of Chambersburg, the nearby county-seat of Franklin, on 30 July 1864.

Chambersburg was the last straw. Continuous raids by the Confederates into south-central Pennsylvania were taking an economic toll, and the citizens had enough. The War, after the Battle of Gettysburg, was turning badly against the Confederates and gave more confidence to the lads from the Union states to join. Locals also feared another large invasion from the Confederates. So, FredM enlisted 3 September 1864 at Gettysburg as a private for one year with a regiment raised in Harrisburg.

Being the oldest son, he had two brothers: David Christian and John Andrew. David registered with the June 1863 Draft, but never served in the war,[202] and John was too young.

He arrived the next day at Camp Curtin, Harrisburg, by now a well organized, bustling "boot camp" for recruits. At muster-in he was described 5 feet 7 inches tall, having hazel eyes, dark hair, and light complexion. After quick training he was assigned to the 100 men making up Company G, 209th Regiment Pennsylvania Volunteer Infantry. That month they shipped south and were with Union forces at Bermuda Hundred, Virginia, on the James River. They were assigned to First Brigade, Third Division, IX Corps.

By March 1864, the successes of General Ulysses S. Grant promoted and transferred him from his western post to taking charge of the eastern war. Grant's successes and command signaled a blow to the Confederates, now seeing an end.

FredM was "present" in the all muster-rolls from 4 September 1864 to his discharge at Alexandria, Virginia, 31 May 1865.

On 17 November 1864, he saw some action when he witnessed his Colonel and Captain, along with 19 other men, captured on the picket line during a Confederate assault.

---

[202] U.S. Civil War Draft Registration Records, 16th Congressional District, Adams County, Pennsylvania.

"The reign of peace on the picket line was over, never to be resumed again, until the bloody 2d of April, 1865 abolished forever the forty-mile cordon of defense stretched in front of the capital of the Rebellion. From the night of the 17th until we finally left the peninsula, there were frequent heavy spats of musketry and almost continuous shelling from the batteries on both sides."[203]

But largely, Fred experienced the mundane army life around Petersburg and Bermuda Hundred. He quickly learned in the hallows of the trenches that hunger sustained the rule "...first duty of a soldier—when hungry loot a sutler; if not hungry, loot him anyhow..."[204]

From September 1864 to April 1865, the unit participated in the siege operation against Petersburg and Richmond. It was 2 April 1865 when the final assault on the 10-month long Siege of Petersburg was executed — a forerunner of trench warfare that would doom many men 53 years later. The regiment lost one officer and four men killed, and two officers and 49 men wounded in the attack. The regiment then began the pursuit of Lee until his surrender.

While posted with his unit at Ft. Steadman, on 25 March 1865, he contracted chronic diarrhea — a typical, but often severe, camp complaint. He also had yellow jaundice and rheumatism (probably hepatitis) and was treated by the regimental surgeon.[205]

These were the closing days of the Civil War. FredM's unit participated in the pursuit of General Lee in the Virginia area. After Lee's surrender in April, the regiment returned to Alexandria on 23 May 1865, and participated in the Grand Review at Washington, D.C., on the 30th.[206]

Fred was officially mustered out at Harrisburg on 31 May 1865 and paid $66.67 bounty enlistment pay, plus $41.56 for a clothing allowance. The regiment lost two officers and 17 enlisted killed; 20 men by disease.[207] In Company G, no deaths but plenty of illness and, eleven men were wounded-in-action out of the 100 souls.

The boredom of the trenches, the stench of illness, and the ugliness of war left an indelible impression on the post-war soldier. And, FredM no longer sat on the sidelines of Adams County society.

---

[203] Barton, Michael. *Glorious Recollections: J. Howard Wert's Lost History of the 209th Regiment, Pennsylvania Volunteer Infantry, 1864-1865...*, 2016. John Howard Wert was Company G's 2nd Lieutenant and enlisted with FredM.

[204] Ibid.

[205] Regimental medical record.

[206] Dyer, page 1625.

[207] Ibid., page 1625.

Paxton Henry Riley (1838-1916)
Woodcut engraving, 1886 History of Adams County...

He had lots of neighbors and kin in Company G namely his brothers-in-laws: First Sergeant Isaac Trimper Riley, Corporal Paxton Henry Riley, Private Hiram David Eshelman (married to his sister Katherine), and John C. Shertzer (married to his sister Maria). Other relatives or relatives-to-be in the future were:

- Andrew A. Bigham.
- Henry J. Beard.
- John Daniel McCarney.
- William Lewis McGlaughlin wounded at Petersburg.
- Joseph W. Rose.
- Anthony G. Sanders and his three brothers.
- Daniel B. Woodring also wounded at Petersburg.

73

John C. Shertzer (1825-1902)
Photograph courtesy Nannie Virginia Shulley

Although never serving in the 165th Infantry, FredM also shared the brotherhood of military experience with members of Company C:

• Brothers-in-law Isaac and Paxton Riley as First Sergeant and Corporal, respectively; but also brother-in-laws Hiram Eshelman and John C. Shertzer.

Other relatives or soon-to-be relatives of some sort were:
• John B. Musselman, Corporal
• John C. Musselman
• George Washington Andrew, later serving with Company I, 210th Pennsylvania Infantry
• Lewis Carbaugh
• 2nd Lt. William Henry Harrison Lowe
• Robert Francis McCleaf
• Henry D. Peters
• Edward M. Riley, a distant cousin to Lucretia, later served with Company I, 3rd Maryland Cavalry
• James Stephen Sanders
• John Jeremiah Sanders
• William Aloysious Sanders, later served with Company A, 91st Pennsylvania Volunteer Infantry Regiment
• Jeremiah Beard Sites
• Thomas James Jefferson Stoops
• David L. Topper

DOMESTIC LIFE

The local newspapers are full of the coming-and-goings of the Shulley's who enjoyed many visitations from their neighbors. Domestic life was a happy one. The devastated county overcame the scars of war to have reunions dances and parties on a routine basis.

FredM continued to prosper, as witnessed by the 1870 Census.[208] By this time, he and Lucretia had four children.

In February 1880, the Shulley's hosted his wife's distant relative, Addie Isadora Nunemaker, marriage in his home to Samuel Keller Hostetter.[209] [210]

---

[208] NARA, 1870, Hamiltonban Township, Adams County, Pennsylvania; M593; Roll 1289; Page 7; Sheet 177A; Line 36-40.

[209] *Intelligencer Journal*, 25 February 1880, page 3.

[210] Samuel never saw military service but was registered with the June 1863 Draft, 9th Congressional District, Manheim Township, Age 21, Miller, unmarried.

In August 1881, the gossipy newspapers reported FredM heading to Kansas.[211] Probably to visit his youngest brother, John Andrew Shulley, who had moved there in 1878 and married Alice Jane Ramp.

Just over 20 years past the end of the Civil War, the populist *1886 History of Adams County* was published with FredM received scant mention under his brother-in-law's accolades,[212] but he was, nevertheless, very well known in the county. Not to be outdone, he apprised to a local newspaper, "Mr. F. Shulley is the possessor of quite a unique relic in the shape of a bottle. It was brought from Germany 150 years ago [1750] by his grandfather."[213]

He appears again in the critical Special Census of 1890 for veterans of the Civil War.[214]

"The U.S. Pension Office requested this special enumeration to help Union veterans locate comrades to testify in pension claims and to determine the number of survivors and widows for pension legislation. (Some congressmen also thought it scientifically useful to know the effect of various types of military service upon veterans' longevity.) To assist in the enumeration, the Pension Office prepared a list of veterans' names and addresses from their files and from available military records held by the U.S. War Department."[215]

In October 1901, the first publicly recorded Shulley family reunion:

"One day last week a party of folks held a family reunion at Tipton's Park, Gettysburg. Among those who comprised the party were: F. Shulley and family, of this place; Mrs. Jacob Hoke and family, of Emmitsburg; Mr. H. F. Shulley and wife, of Reading; Lillie R. and Meta Shulley and wife [sic], of Womelsdorf. A very pleasant day was spent."[216,217]

PENSION BUSINESS

At age 53, FredM started to feel his bones and applied for his first federal pension in early February 1890, per The Dependent

---

[211] *Gettysburg Star & Sentinel*, 3 August 1881, page 3.

[212] *1886 History of Adams County...* pages 446, 471.

[213] Adams County Independent, page 8.

[214] 1890 US Special Census Schedule. Hamiltonban Township, Adams County, Pennsylvania; Enumeration District 13; Line 42.

[215] United States, "1890 'Veterans Census,' www.census.gov/history/www/genealogy/decennial_census_records/1890_veterans_census.html

[216] *Adams County Independent*, 8 October 1902, page 3.

[217] Another claimed "first" reunion was held 25 June 1939. *Gettysburg Times*, 3 July 1939, page 3.

Pension Act. On 21 February the Bureau of Pensions verified his illnesses contracted while in the service.[218]

He received his federal pension on 4 July 1898, and returned a questionnaire on his family, and, again on 4 May 1899.[219]

Aging and poorer, he and Lucretia are found, in their 50s and 60s, in the 1900 U.S. Census.[220]

February 1903: The Pension Office grants FredM, $8.[221] March: Pension granted for $8.[222]

The Act of February 6, 1907 permitted him to file for another pension on 22 February 1907. The filing was witnessed by Jacob Musselman and G. W. McGlaughlin, both of Fairfield, and sworn before D. P. Musselman, Justice of-the-Peace.[223]

GENERAL HEALTH

FredM's health was generally good during this Gilded Age, but he did have some incidences of concern:

"Several weeks ago [December 1878] Frederick Shully, [sic] of Hamiltonban township, made a narrow escape from serious injury and possible death. He was hauling [contracted railroad] rails from the mountain, and in coming down a steep hill, he undertook to put his foot on the break, slipped and feel [sic] under the wagon, the hind wheel clogging on his breast and shoulder, The horse was a quiet one and instantly stopped on Mr. S. hollering to him. James Watson was cutting timber close by and attracted by Mr. S's cries went to his relief, backing the horse and relieving him from his dangerous position. Mr. S. was somewhat bruised about the shoulder, but its all right again."[224]

And in August 1896: "We are very sorry to say that Mr. Frederick Shulley, one of our rushing butchers, and, also, correspondent for the 'Littlestown Independent,' is now lying in a very critical condition from the effects of a very hard kick in the hand from a very bad

---

[218] Pension record. NARA.

[219] Ibid.

[220] NARA, Hamiltonban Township, Adams County, Pennsylvania; T623; Roll 1354; Sheet 11B; Page 217/218; Line 100/1-6.

[221] *New Oxford Item*, New Oxford, newspaper, Adams County, Pennsylvania, 20 February 1903, page 13.

[222] *Gettysburg Compiler*, 4 March 1903, page 2.

[223] Pension record, NARA.

[224] *Gettysburg Complier*, 2 January 1879, page 2.

steer. At least he is lying—whether critical or not, and we hope his recovery will be speedy, for he is a good fellow."[225]

October 1897: "Mr. F. Shulley who has been suffering with blood-poison in his hand has nearly recovered."[226]

October 1899: "On Thursday of last week as Mr. F. Shulley, of this place, was picking apples, the ladder turned and threw Mr. Shully [sic] heavily to the ground, a distance of 12 feet. The gentleman fell on his back which was considerably bruised but at this writing is again able to be about."[227]

Wife Lucretia also had her ailments: "Mrs. F. Shulley, who went to the hospital on the 17th of January for treatment, and who had an operation performed, is improving slowly. She is now able to be about, and has left the hospital, and is staying with her children."[228]

POLITICS

FredM, like many returning vets from war, dabbled in local politics. In March 1867, he was elected Hamiltonban Township Supervisor.[229] In March 1883, he was the Hamiltonban Township road auditor, noting a settled account with supervisor Anthony G. Sanders, another war veteran.[230] In February 1896, he was the Adams County Inspector, 1896.[231] In September 1903, he was elected vice-president of the Adams County, Pennsylvania Republican Club, finally concluding his active political career.[232]

GRAND ARMY OF THE REPUBLIC

FredM's most most impressing social post-war activity was undoubtedly his participation in the Grand Army of the Republic (GAR). The GAR was a fraternal organization founded in 1866 composed of veterans of the Union Army and Navy. It quickly grew throughout the country. It became an advocacy force in politics, promoting patriotic education, lobbying for pensions, and helped make Memorial Day ("Decoration Day") a national holiday. They also sponsored "camps" — meetings of veterans, at times real camped-in-the-field. Today, the GAR is akin to groups like the

---

[225] *Gettysburg Star & Sentinel,* 18 August 1896, page 3.

[226] *Adams County Independent*, 9 October 1897, page 1.

[227] Ibid., 7 October 1899, page 4.

[228] Ibid., 14 March 1903, page 1.

[229] *Adams Sentinel,* 26 March 1867, page 4.

[230] *Gettysburg Compiler,* 28 March 1883, page 3.

[231] "Election Returns." *Adams County Independent,* 29 February 1896, page 2.

[232] *Gettysburg Compiler,* 2 September 1903, page 3.

American Legion. Dissolved in 1956, the GAR's legal successor is the Sons of Union Veterans of the Civil War.

In April 1891, FredM became Commander of the GAR post, James Dixon number 83 — a high honor with many veterans in the county.[233] The lane to his farm was homaged "Shulley lane."[234] And again elected in December 1895.[235] In June 1897, "Mr. Frederick Shulley was at Johnstown last week attending the State encampment."[236]

Familiar names found in the October 1902 encampment:

"Among the veterans and their relatives who are attending the G. A. R. encampment at Washington this week are the following: Washington Irving, Mr. and Mrs. Nicholas Wierman, Hon. W. T. Ziegler, W. E. Zielgler, H. G. Blair, John McMannus, John Toot, Samuel Andrews, Jacob Eckenrode, Harry Little, Wm. H. Frock, Wm. Rupp, of Gettysburg; C. P. K. Walter, Wm. Bream, of Biglerville; John Fiddler, Chas. Rhodes, Harry Hartzel, Wesley Oyler and Geo. W. Routzahn, of Biglerville; Isaiah Test, of Bendersville; Samuel Humes, William Bowers and Joseph Ziegler, of Idaville; P. S. Harbaugh, John F. Low, Adam Snyder, Jas. Mickley, Geo. Seitz, Howard Moore, Fred. Shulley, Samuel Walter, Paxton Riley and wife and Dave Riley[237] and son, of Fairfield."[238]

In December 1899, FredM was elected by the James Dixon Post 83, G.A.R, as Delegate to Encampment.[239] And again in 1903, he was elected, Assistant Inspector, District 24, GAR.[240]

January 1905: "Last week Mr. F. Shully [sic] installed the officers of James Dixon Post, No., 83, Commander, Wm. H. Low; Senior Commander, John Strausbaugh; Jr. Vice Commander, Samuel Walter; Officer of the Day, James Mickley; Officer of the Guard, P. H. Riley; Quartermast., T. H. Moore; Chaplain, John Manherz; Adju-

[233] *Gettysburg Star & Sentinel,* 28 April 1891, page 3.

[234] *Adams County Independent,* 15 August 1891, page 1.

[235] *Gettysburg Compiler,* 24 December 1895, page 2.

[236] *Gettysburg Star & Sentinel,* 8 June 1897, page 2.

[237] David Alexander Riley (1835-1908), registered for the Draft but never was called-up to serve.

[238] *Gettysburg Compiler*, 8 October 1902, page 3.

[239] *Adams County Independent,* 2 December 1899, page 1.

[240] *Proceedings of the 37th Annual Encampment of the Department of Pennsylvania Grand Army of the Republic at Allentown, June 3d and 4th, 1903.* Harrisburg, Pennsylvania: Wm. Stanley Ray, State Printer of Pennsylvania, 1908. Page 30.

Estray Heifer.

CAME to the residence of the subscriber, 1 mile south of Fairfield, about the 10th of July, last, a

RED MOOLEY HEIFER, supposed to be about 3 years old. The owner is desired to come forward, prove property, pay charges and take her away.

FREDERICK SHULLEY.

Sept. 8.—3t*

Adams County Sentinel and General Advertiser, Gettysburg, Pennsylvania, 8 September 1863, page 3.

tant, John F. Low; Sergeant. A. G. Sanders; Delegate to Encampment, F. Shulley Alternate, S. Walter.[241]

June 1905: "Frederick Shulley has gone to Reading as a delegate to the G. A. R. Encampment which convenes at that place this week."[242]

Although not GAR related, in May 1908, with many familiar names:

"FAIRFIELD VETS OF THE 209th. Names of Those Living and of Those Who No More Answer Roll-Call.

Fairfield, May 22—Many of The Independent's readers may be interested in knowing the names of the boys who volunteered to serve in Company G, 209th Regt. Penna. Vol., whose address was Fairfield at time of enlistment. They were: Paxton H. Riley, I. Trimper Riley, J. C. Shertzer, Hiram Eshelman, Wm. Metz, Fred. Shulley, John Kint, Joseph Rose Daniel Woodring, Wm. Boiler Lewis McGlaughlin, Wilson Eyler, Lewis Butt, John Moser, Thomas Culbertson, James McCullough, Daniel Biesecker, Thomas Winebrenner, Jos. Bowling, Henry Beard, Wm. Yingling, Shields Hunter, Peter Brooks, Joshua Cease, Charles Hinkle, Wash. Culbertson, John Smith, John W. Baker, C. H. Walter.

The following have died since the war: Hiram Eshelman, J. C. Shertzer, John Kint, Thomas Culbertson, James McCullough,

---

[241] *Adams County Independent,* 21 January 1905, page 1.
[242] Ibid., 10 June 1905, page 8.

Charles Hinkle, Thomas Winebreuner, John W. Baker, Daniel Biesecker, Joseph Bowling, John Smith, Joshua Cease.

A great many from Littlestown and other places were in the 209th Regiment."[243]

At age 68, 1905 seemed to be the end of FredM's activity with the GAR.

BUSINESS

Life with FredM was filled with business activities. In June 1877, the industrious fellow "…built a new house near his limekiln last summer, and this spring has put up a small barn."[244]

His business activities naturally centered around his farm, focused on the creamery and butchering enterprises.

Active in collecting milk cream from other farmers, at age 54, "Mr. F. Shulley who gathers cream for the Greenridge creamery paid 16 cents for cream last week."[245] "Last Tuesday F. Shulley lost an eight gallon can of milk from his wagon. If anyone has found the can, Mr. Shulley would be much obliged for its return.[246] "Chas. Corwell found the cream can which F. Shulley recently lost from his wagon. He promptly returned it to the owner, for which he has the thanks of Mr. Shulley."[247] "Mr. F. Shulley, of this place, who has been handling cream for the past nine years, intends starting a creamery and will have a cream separator in working order at or near Fairfield in the near future."[248]

In March 1902: "Mr. F. Shulley, of this place, intends assisting Mr. C. A. Spangler in the butcher business, next summer, with headquarters at Blue Ridge Summit."[249] And in the following year, "F. Shulley of this place, who is in the butchering business at Ringgold, has been standing in the Cash Supply Meat Store in Waynesboro for the last couple of weeks."[250]

FredM was not afraid to diversify his business interests. In January 1907, "The Pure Oil Company are hauling pipes along the land of Grove's. They have pipes placed through F. Shulley's and part of

243 Ibid., 23 May 1908, page 6.

244 *Gettysburg Star & Sentinel,* 14 June 1877, page 3.

245 *Adams County Independent,* 3 October 1891, page 1.

246 Ibid., 8 February 1896, page 1.

247 Ibid., 15 February 1896, page 1.

248 Ibid., 11 June 1898, page 4.

249 Ibid., 1 March 1902, page 1.

250 Ibid., 14 March 1903, page 1.

New Advertisements.

Mr. F, Shulley, of Fairfield, has the latest in milk churns. See business locals on last page.

Any person wanting a first class churn, one of the latest improved machines, can be accommodated by calling on F. Shulley, or near Fairfield, he will sell and deliver the churn at a moderate rate.

Adams County Independent, 17 August 1895, pages 1, 4.

D. C. Shulley's[251] farms in Hamiltonban township."[252] (Which, later, nearly killed his great-nephew, John Calvin Shulley, in a dynamite accident in February.[253])

And with a boast, "Mr. F. Shulley has a pumpkin vine measuring 162 feet, the longest vine, from root, measuring 51 feet."[254]

He invited a local veterinary, Dr. William G. Dubs, to live on his farm in exchange for some services. Dr. Dubs served in Company K, 87th Pennsylvania Volunteer Infantry, enlisting late in the war, 17 March 1865, but may have bumped into FredM at the Siege of Petersburg.

"Dr. W. G. Dubs moved from Fairfield to F. Shulley's house in the country."[255] At least part of the arrangement was positive as "Dr. W. G. Dubbs, who lives in the F. Shulley property, presented Mr. Shulley with a pumpkin of the Roosevelt variety, that weighed 113 pound."[256]

"Veterinary W. G. Dubs reports a great many sick horses in this neighborhood. Some have the distemper. F. Shulley had a horse that had distemper very bad, but the Doctor brought it round all right."[257]

---

[251] FredM's brother, David Christian Shulley.

[252] *Adams County Independent,* 26 January 1907, page 1.

[253] *Gettysburg Compiler,* 6 February 1907, page 8.

[254] *Adams County Independent*, 5 September 1895, page 4.

[255] Ibid., 9 April 1904, page 6.

[256] Ibid., 14 October 1905, page 5.

[257] Ibid., 20 March 1897, page 1.

And, the gossipy local newspapers reported many business trips of an unknown nature with his brother-in-law: "F. Shulley and P. H. Reiley [sic] made a business trip to Emmitsburg last week..."[258] "Messers A. Grove and F. Shulley, of this place, made a business trip to Waynesboro, this week."[259] "Messrs F. Shulley and P. H. Riley made a business trip to Gettysburg last Saturday."[260] "F. Shulley made a business trip to Gettysburg last Monday."[261]

But in March 1896, FredM needed some cash: "Robert Sanders has bought two acres of land lying along the West Fairfield road, from Frederick Shulley. He expects to build a house on it in the near future."[262] Robert was married to FredM's niece, Mary Jane Shertzer, John C. Shertzer's daughter.

FredM's cozy relationship with the free press ended in March 1895:

"I was sorry that I could not have a longer talk with our wide-a-wake correspondent, Maj. [sic] Fred Shulley. The gentleman is a hustler in the news gathering line, and *The Independent* owes much to his untiring efforts in behalf of the paper."[263]

Wife Lucretia had times of merry in her life:

"Mrs. F. Shulley was agreeably surprised on Friday evening, Sept. 4th, to find a host of her friends and neighbors gather at her home to congratulate her on her 52nd birthday. The evening was spent in pleasant conversation and the young folks sowed their 'wild oats' and indulged in other games. About ten o'clock the guests were ushered around a table well filled with all and everything the season could afford. Cakes of every description, ice cream and lemonade were served and after all had done justice to the good things, they retired to an adjoining room. Mrs. Shully was the recipient of some valuable presents, one of which was a cane-seat rocking chair. Mrs. Shulley extended her sincere thanks to all for their kindness. After wishing Mrs. Shulley long life and happy days, they all returned to their homes saying they had a good time. Those present were Henry M. Sanders and wife, Ruel Musselman and wife, Millard Stoner and wife, P. H. Riley and wife, Dr. W. G. Dubs and wife and son David, Andy Weikert and wife, Joe H. Creager and wife, D. C. Stoner and wife, Christy Frey and wife, D. B. Riley, wife and daughter Mary, John Manherz, John Musselman and wife, J. J. Reindollar and wife, J.

---

[258] Ibid., 27 April 1895, page 1.

[259] Ibid., 7 September 1895, page 1.

[260] Ibid., 18 November 1899, page 1.

[261] Ibid., 25 May 1907, page 1.

[262] Ibid., 28 March 1896, page 4.

[263] Ibid., 9 March 1895, page 3.

C. Shertzer and wife, Mrs. Andy Musselman, Mrs. S. Firor, C. P. Bream and wife, Samuel Walters and wife, Milton Butt and wife, Mrs. A. Grove, Mrs. John Butt, Mrs. Lucinda Musselman, Lieut. C. J. Sefton, Dick Polly, Effie Walter, James White, Ada Harbaugh, Clara Musselman, Nevin Spangler, George Neely, Lottie M. Shulley, John O. Musselman, Mettie Marshall, Harry Brown, Clara Donaldson, Harry Walter, Mrs. Charlotte Manherz, Bessie Plank, Marshall Brown, Dora Harbolt, Mary Warrick, Parke L. Shulley, J. Lowry Hill, Gertie Bream, Mrs. Elliotte, Elmer Mondorff, Robert Watson, Ivan Riley, Gross Beaver, Cordelia Musselman, Fannie Lowe, Charles Glenn, Ruth Riley, Doll Sefton, Harvey Sanders."[264]

Always active in the community with her husband, "The Lutheran Mite Society met at Mrs. F. Shulley's on last Tuesday. They have their receipt and cook book ready for sale. Every family should have one of these books."[265]

Lucretia, in 1905, was reported to have the largest tomatoes in town.[266]

THE END IS NEAR

Advancing years started to make themselves noticed. In 1908: "Mrs. F. Shulley, while walking on the icy pavements last Saturday, slipped and fell, striking her wrist on a curb stone and bruising it considerable.[267] ...but cannot use her hand as yet.[268] ...and still wears the shingle on her arm."[269]

Now in their twilight years, FredM and Lucretia are found in the April 1910 census.[270] That June, son "Harry F. Shulley, of 1650 Muhlenberg street, [Reading] spent two weeks the guest of his father, Frederick Shulley, Gettysburg, who is quite ill."[271] A month later, "Frederick Shulley, an aged gentleman of this place and a veteran of the Civil War, is seriously ill at his home on Centennial street [Gettysburg]."[272] In October, "Frederick Shulley and wife have quit house-keeping and have taken up their residence with their daughter,

---

[264] Ibid., 12 September 1896, page 4.

[265] Ibid., 10 December 1904, page 1.

[266] Ibid., 12 August 1905, page 5.

[267] Ibid., 18 January 1908, page1.

[268] Ibid., 25 January 1908, page 1.

[269] Ibid., 1 February 1908, page 1.

[270] Fairfield, Adams County, Pennsylvania; NARA T624; Roll 1292; Enumeration District 15; Sheet 3B "Water Street," Line 58-59.

[271] *Reading Times,* newspaper, Reading, Berks County, Pennsylvania. 13 June 1910, page 7.

[272] Adams County Independent, *23 July 1910, page 1.*

Mrs. Jennie Hafer, at Womelsdorf."[273] But residing with the Hafer's didn't work out and, shortly thereafter, "Frederick Shulley and wife have quit housekeeping and have gone to Chambersburg to live with

Lucretia Virginia Shulley, *nee* Riley (1844-1922)
Photograph courtesy of Nannie Virginia Shulley

[273] *Gettysburg Star & Sentinel,* 26 October 1910, page 3.

their daughter, Mrs. Harvey Sanders[274] and, "...has been an invalid for some time."[275]

The U.S. Pension office succinctly reported:

"S.9628. Frederick Shulley served as a private in Company G, Two hundred and ninth Regiment Pennsylvania Volunteer Infantry, from September 3, 1864, to May 31, 1865, and was honorably discharged. He is a pensioner under the service act of February 6, 1907, at the rate of $15 per month. He was formerly pensioned under the act of June 27, 1890, at $10 per month. His claim under the general law, filed in December, 1889, was rejected in May, 1891, because of no record or other evidence to show incurrence of rheumatism in the service.

The claimant is now about 74 years of age. His last medical examination by a board of surgeons, June 21, 1905, showed that he was afflicted with rheumatism and heart disease and was in feeble health from the infirmities incident to old age, and practically unable to perform manual labor.

Medical evidence filed with this committee shows that claimant is now suffering from progressive spastic paralysis, and that he is entirely helpless, requiring the same attention as an infant. Neighbors testify that claimant is a helpless and infirm invalid, unable to stand or walk, and is dependent upon others for a living. An increase in soldier's pension to $24 per month is recommended on the ground of his present condition; it is not due to his service, which was less than one year, and no greater increase is warranted."[276]

July 1911: "Frederick Shulley, a former resident of this place, is seriously ill at his home in Chambersburg."[277] But, by 12 August, Frederick M. Shulley passed away at age 74 years, five months and twenty-one days. The local newspapers memorialized his passing:[278]

"Frederick Shulley a veteran of the Civil War died at the home of his son-in-law, Harvey Sanders, at the corner of Fourth and Market streets at 6:15 o'clock on Saturday morning. Mr. Shulley had

---

[274] *Gettysburg Times,* 28 October 1910, page 1.

[275] *Gettysburg Compiler,* 9 November 1910, page 16.

[276] *United States Congressional Serial Set, 61st Congress, 3d Session, December 5, 1910 - March 4, 1911.* Senate Reports, Washington: Government Printing office, 1911. Volume B, page 46.

[277] *Gettysburg Star & Sentinel,* 19 July 1911, page 2.

[278] *Adams County News,* Gettysburg, Adams County, Pennsylvania, 19 August 1911, page 1; *Adams County Independent,* 19 August 1911, page 2, 5; *Democratic Advocate,* Westminster, Frederick County, Maryland, 25 August 1911, page 1; *Public Opinion,* 14 August 1911, page 1; *Valley Spirit,* 16 August 1911, page 5; *Gettysburg Compiler,* 23 August 1911, page 7.

been an invalid for about three years. He was aged 74 years, 5 months and 22 days.

Surviving are his wife and these children: Mrs. Howard Hafer of Womelsdorf; Mrs. Simon Mower of Womelsdorf; Mrs. Harvey Sanders of Chambersburg; Mrs. Chas Reed of Fairfield; Harry Shulley of Reading; Charles Shulley of Reading; Mrs. S. White Plank of Union Bridge, and Parke Shulley of Reading.

Funeral services will be held at the home of his son-in-law this evening at 7:30 o'clock and the remains will be taken to Fairfield, Adams County, on Tuesday morning where interment will be made."

Four days after his death, his widow, Lucretia, filed for a pension witnessed by John F. Law and Charles F. Hoffman.[279] FredM's sister, Maria H. Shertzer, then age 78, and Miss Kate Kready, age 77, both of Fairfield, filed an affidavit on behalf of the widow stating that they were witnesses at the marriage of the Shulley's.[280]

On 3 October 1911, Dr. Guy P. Asper, of Drs. Asper and Fairfax G. Wright of 153 South Main Street, Chambersburg, certified in a letter to the U.S. Pension Office that FredM had died of "...Asthenia following Erysepelas [sic]. Frederick Shulley was invaleded for a number of years by a progressive Spastic Paralyses." Roughly, death was due to a deep infectious skin inflamation caused by strep poisoning, weakening the body.[281]

Lucretia, passed away eleven years later at the Hafer's house on 30 August 1922, in Berks County, but not before writing her Last Will and Testament. She was subsequently dropped from the pension rolls, but had been receiving a monthly pension of $30.[282]

"Word has been received here of the death in Womelsdorr, [sic] Wednesday of Mrs. Frederick Shulley, a former resident of Fairfield. She was born near Fairfield on September 4, 1844 and was a charter member of the Fairfield Lutheran church. She was aged 77 years, 11 months and 26 days.

She is survived by the following children: Mrs. H. M. Hafer, and Mrs. H. T. Moyer, of Womelsdorff; Mrs. H. F. Sanders, of Harrisburg; H. F. Shulley; E. M. Shulley, and P. L. Shulley, of Reading. Fourteen grandchildren and 9 great-grandchildren also survive."[283]

---

[279] Pension record. NARA. 16 August 1911.

[280] Ibid.

[281] Ibid. Also, his death record, File number 73870 with the Commonwealth of Pennsylvania.

[282] Ibid.

[283] *Gettysburg Times*, 1 September 1922, page 1.

The children of Fred and Lucretia went onward in time in prosperity with little tumult:

i.   Jennie Amanda (1863-1927) married Howard M. Hafer (1864-1950), and they owned the Seltzer House, a boarding business in Womelsdorf, for many years. They had two children.

ii.   Lillie Riley (1866-1945) married Simon Peter Moyer (1854-1946), and they also lived in Womelsdorf. She had one daughter previous to her marriage to Simon, but between Simon and her, they had two children.

iii. Emma Maria (1867-1875) died, age 7.

iv.   Mary Etta (1870-1933) married Harvey Francis Sanders (1870-1944). They had seven children and produced a large brood of descendants in the south-central Pennsylvania area.

v.   Dora Euphema (1871-1918) married Charles Francis Reed (1872-1945), and they lived in the Adams County area. They had twelve children.

vi.   Harry Frederick (1874-1950) married Flora Anna *nee* Hoke (1874-1952), and they resided in the Reading area. At one time, he was a policeman in Reading. They had two children.

vii. Charles Meade (1877-1947) married Mary Erma *nee* Musselman (1880-1949), and also resided in the Reading area. They had three children. One daughter, Nannie Virginia Shulley (1904-1998), graciously supplied much information on the Shulley clan.

viii. Lottie May (1881-1919) married Sentman White Plank (1876-1960), a butcher, also in the Reading area. They had four children.

ix.   Parke Luther (1883-1960) married Mary Elizabeth *nee* Seiders (1877-1960), they also resided in metropolitan Reading and had no children.

So, what was FredM's middle name? All official records always note "M." A newspaper notice on the marriage of his granddaughter Meta Ray Shulley, she was erroneously called the "daughter of Frederick **Mayer** Shelley."[284] This is the only place a full middle name is found. Traditionally, in the context of the era, middle names were usually taken from relatives. None can be found with names starting with "M." Unless there is a collaborating document, his middle name shall remain "M."

---

[284] *The Record*, newspaper, Hackensack, New Jersey, 15 May 1925, page 4. Also, *The Courier Post*, newspaper, Camden, New Jersey, 16 May 1925, page 1.

Frederick M. Shulley (1837-1911)
Photograph courtesy of Nannie Virginia Shulley

```
┌─────────────────┐
│ Peter SANDERS   │──┐   ┌──────────────────┐
│ (1720- ca 1767) │  ├───│ Anna Regina ____ │
└─────────────────┘  │   └──────────────────┘
                     │
        ┌─────────────────┐   ┌──────────────────┐
        │ Peter SANDERS   │───│ Susanna KUNNE    │
        │ (bef. 1756-1817)│   │ (1749-ca 1832)   │
        └─────────────────┘   └──────────────────┘
                     │
         ┌─────────────────┐   ┌──────────────────┐
         │ Adam J. SANDERS │───│ Susanna TOPPER   │
         │ (1800-1863)     │   │ (1803-1895)      │
         └─────────────────┘   └──────────────────┘
                     │
          ┌───────────────────┐   ┌────────────────────────┐
          │ Anthony G. SANDERS│───│ Mary Catharine DICK    │
          │ (1833-1911)       │   │ (1835-1905)            │
          └───────────────────┘   └────────────────────────┘
```

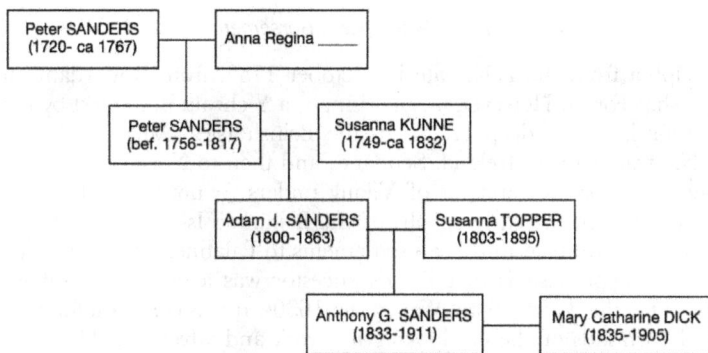

V. "These Magnificent Horsemen..."

Anthony G. Sanders, son of Adam J. Sanders (1800-1863) and Susanna Topper (1803-1895), was born on 26 November 1833, probably on the farm in Liberty Township in Adams County, Pennsylvania,[285] and baptized in Emmitsburg, Frederick County, Maryland, on 2 February 1834, in Saint Josephs Roman Catholic Church, the nearest Catholic Church at the time.[286,287] The origin of "G" in his name Anthony "G" Sanders is unknown. He rarely used this middle initial on any documents. "G" is first found in some of his children's marriage records, in his 1890 and 1910 Censuses, a 1905 newspaper accounts of "A. G. Sanders," and on his death record. A few Internet sources creatively claim it is "George" or even "Gregory," but there is no evidence of his middle name. Therefore, it remains herein as "G."

Anthony came from a long line of hard-working folks. His great-grandfather, Peter Sanders I (1720-c1767), and wife Anna Regina (her maiden name unknown at this time, but believed to be Achenbach) were German-speaking immigrants. Peter arrived in Phil-

---

[285] The Adam J. Sanders family, in 1840, was residing in the township. 1840 US Census, NARA Roll 435; Page 20A.

[286] St. Joseph Roman Catholic Church, Emmitsburg, Frederick County, Maryland.

[287] Rose, Albert Louis, *York, York County, Pennsylvania: notebook.* "Sanders Gen. General Info & sources of Peter Sanders Family." Pennsylvania church records of Saint Mary's Catholic, Fairfield, Adams County, Saint Rita Catholic, Blue Ridge Summit, Franklin County; Saint Johns Lutheran Church, Fairfield, Adams County, Saint Josephs Cemetery, Emmitsburg, Frederick County, Maryland, The Pines Church, New Chester, Pennsylvania, Saint Francis Xavier Catholic Cemetery, Gettysburg, Adams County, Pennsylvania." Page 13.

adelphia from the Palatinate in October 1752, from Rotterdam on the ship Forest. However, unsurprisingly, a Y-chromosome test by the author indicates deep origins in the British Isles. An even deeper DNA trail leads to Ireland, Scotland, and then to Norway and Sweden, probably descendants of Viking raiders — not unusual for the occurrence in the early epochs of the Britannic Islands. So, why go from northwestern European settlements to Palatine, Germany? The current hypothesis is that Peter's ancestor was a mercenary soldier hired for the Thirty Years War in the 1630s. It was common for Scot and Irish lads of the era looking for work and adventure. However, this is for discussion at another future time.

Nevertheless, son, Peter II (born before 1756-died 1817), was a pivotal progeny who, with his wife, Susanna Kunne (1749-ca 1832), made an impressive mark on south-central Pennsylvania, leaving over 10,000 known descendants across the country at the time of this essay. Their namesakes remain in Adams County, Pennsylvania, even today.

Peter II was the father of Adam J. Sanders[288] (1800-1863) who married Susanna Topper (1803-1895). Adam quietly labored in the fields of the county. Susanna's grandfather, Andrew Topper (1747-1831), served in the Revolutionary War as a Captain in the Sixth Battalion Northampton Company Militia, 4th Company.[289]

In the *antebellum* of the Civil War, Adams's son, Anthony G. Sanders, first shows up officially in the 1850 Census as a 16-year-old laborer on his father's farm.[290] Ten years later, in 1860, he is living with his bride and firstborn in her fathers house in the township next door, again as a "laborer."[291] The farm just southeast of Fairfield, east of the hill north of Jack's Mountain. His neighbor, Frederick M. Shulley, was just on the other side of the peak.

Anthony married the farm girl-next-door, Mary Catharine *nee* Dick,[292] daughter of a state militiaman and county auditor Capt. Peter

---

[288] The "J" middle initial only shows up on his tombstone and son Anthony's death record. Some Internet sources and websites claim the "J" stands for "Jeremiah" or even "Joseph," but it is nowhere to be found, to date, after nearly 45 years of research by the author.

[289] *Pennsylvania State Archives*, Pennsylvania State Library, Harrisburg, Pennsylvania. 5th Series, Vol. I, p. 3862; 7th Series Volume V, page 354. "Andre Dapper."

[290] Liberty Township, Adams County, Pennsylvania. NARA M432; Roll 743; Page 134A.

[291] 1860 US Census, Hamiltonban Township, Adams County, Pennsylvania. NARA M653; Roll 1057; Page: 251.

[292] The only time her middle name "Catharine" was used was in her husband's military pension record, 4 July 1898. Otherwise, it was always "C."

Dick (1811-1891) and his wife Harriet *nee* Lau (1807-1881). Anthony and Mary were married by Father Micheal Dougherty on 18 January 1858, in the Roman Catholic mission church at Fairfield.[293]

By October 1869, Anthony was elected School Director for Hamiltonban Township,[294] having a vested interest of his now five children:

i. Peter Joseph (1859-1936), who married Mary Ellen "Martha" Staley (1862-1932)

ii. George Edward (1860-1940); married May Elizabeth Butt (1868-1931)

iii. John Elmer (1862-1937); married Margaret L. Quinn (1871-1918), and then secondly Lou Frances Newans (1972-1955)

iv. Harriet Sara or "Hallie" (1866-1952); married John A. Hoffman (1866-1911)

v. James Samuel (1868-1958); married Lucy Susan McCleaf (1875-1935)

By the time he was Hamiltonban Township road auditor in March 1883,[295] the rest of his children were born:

vi. Harvey Francis (1870-1944), who married Mary Etta Shulley, daughter of Frederick M. Shulley, in the previously cited chapter.

vii. Edward Charles (1875-1952); married Florence E. Hardman (1884-1959)

viii. Mary Margaret (1878-1961); married James Oliver Peters (1871-1953)

ix. Harry Leo (1879-1958), first married his cousin Catherine Louise Sanders (1884-1928), then Margaret C. Woodring (1913-1952), another cousin.

Anthony and Mary were active in the Catholic Church all their lives. Indeed, in 1885:

"Thos. A. Fitzgerald writes to Father Reiter at Conewago, from Fairfield, Adams County, Pennsylvania, Aug. 31st, 1858: says congregation is very anxious that one of the Conewago Fathers attend their church, and they will make every effort to pay off the debt and make up something for the pastor …names of families of the congregation: Jesse P. Topper, Adam Sanders … Gregory Topper … James,

---

293 *Bureau of Pension questionnaire, 4 July 1898.*
294 *Gettysburg Star & Sentinel,* 29 October 1869, page 1.
295 *Gettysburg Compiler,* 28 March 1883, page 1.

Anthony and Peter Sanders, Peter Dick ... Mrs. Peters ... Andrew, Charles and widow of John Sanders ..."296

ANTHONY GOES TO WAR

Anthony was 29 years of age when the first Confederate raids intruded into the area in October 1862. He was a young father with small children at the time. He kept a low-profile on any commitment to military enlistment, but law-abiding, he did register for the June 1863 Draft.297

The early 1860s were dangerous times for the people in southern Pennsylvania, with Confederate raids, the Battle of Gettysburg in 1863, and theft of property and harassment left physical and psychological marks. Anthony did not enlist into the Union army until 29 February of 1864, in Chambersburg, during a recruitment drive. He was influenced by General Ulysses S. Grant, newly appointed commander in chief of all Union armies. Grant's successes bolstered morale in the North, and trust from the foot soldier. General William Tecumseh Sherman was also making great successes in Mississippi; Union forces entered Jacksonville, Florida and, 109 Union officers escaped the infamous Libby Prison with tales of horror.

A "Laborer," described as having blue eyes and of "ruddy" or florid complexion standing five feet eleven and one-half inches tall. He enlisted into newly formed Company 'L' of the Twenty-second Regiment Pennsylvania Cavalry given $300 to join plus another $60 on 9 March as a local bounty pay (accredited to Hamiltonban Township, Adams County, Pennsylvania). He signed up for three years service. The regiment was also called the 185th Volunteers because of the six-month enlisted men, mostly dismounted cavalry.

The regiment formed with the consolidation of two battalions, the Old Ringgold Cavalry and Company G "the LaFayette" Calvary raised during the Gettysburg Campaign.298 Also, the Washington County Cavalry Companies B, C, E, and F added.299 Jacob C. Higgins, a seasoned veteran, was selected to serve as colonel, A. J. Greenfield as lieutenant colonel, and George T. Work, Elias S. Troxell, and

---

296 Reily, John Timon, Conewago, *A Collection of Catholic Local History Gathered From the Field of Catholic Missionary Labor Within Our Reach.* Martinsburg, West Virginia: Herald Printing, 1885, Page 188.

297 Civil War Draft Registration, June 1863, Hamiltonban Township, Adams County, Pennsylvania, 16th Congressional District, page 119; age 29, white, laborer, married, born in Pennsylvania.

298 National Parks Service. www.nps.gov/civilwar/search-battle-units-detail.htm?battleUnitCode=UPA0022RC01

299 PA-Roots, Inc. www.pa-roots.com/pacw/cavalry/22ndcav3yrs/22ndcavorg.html

Henry A. Myers as majors. Anthony's Company L's Captain was William A. Sands and had many recruits from Berks County of which Anthony met three other "Sanders" fellows, unrelated to him.

Soon after his enlistment, the unit moved out on 1 March 1864 to Martinsburg, West Virginia, for training and then later on to Cumberland, Maryland. In April, 700 of the unmounted men proceeded to the Remount Camp, Pleasant Valley, Maryland, receiving horses and equipment, drill, and discipline.[300] From 30 April to 16 May 1864, his unit left for the New Market Expedition in Virginia.

Anthony's unit joined other Union units at Siegel's Expedition from Martinsburg to Lost River Gap to Lynchburg to New Market, Virginia, by 15 May. They met severe opposition from the Confederates, resulting in a retreat. Later, regrouped, they took Lynchburg in an expedition beginning 26 May to 1 July 1864. The purpose of the expedition was to cut off the Confederate line of supply. However, because of low ammunition and supplies themselves, they were forced to retreat to the West Virginian mountains, guarding the small supplies they had left. Colonel Harry Ward Gilmor (1838-1883), a Maryland partisan Confederate, attacked this Union supply train and destroyed it. Anthony was most certainly involved in this action.

By 1864, the War was much more personal, and it became more intense with Union troops putting pressure on the rebels with scorched-earth policies. Col. Gilmor, and his 3,000 troops, doggedly attacked Anthony and his Union comrades in Maryland and Virginia weeks before the Burning of Chambersburg.

As the Union infantry fell back to the West Virginian Mountains, Anthony's unit fell back to the operations at Harper's Ferry, before Confederates advancing upon Martinsburg (2 July 1864). The unit was guarding considerable supplies at Martinsburg, but seeing an advancing superior force, they took what they could carry and moved to Harper's Ferry by 4 July. Seeing the possibility of being trapped there, they moved to Maryland Heights and Hagerstown, Maryland, by 6-7 July.

The Confederate forces continued to advance in parties, and entered Hagerstown at the same time (6-7 July) and commenced to pillage it. The Union forces continued to be spread out, bottled-up and, tactically neutralized at Maryland Heights. Anthony's unit, by 22 July 1864, had moved back to Pleasant Valley, Maryland. But soon, his unit and infantry units pushed an attack on the Confederate forces near Winchester, Virginia (near Kernsville). Unfortunately, they were beaten and forced to retreat to Martinsburg in a terrible

---

[300] CivilWarIndex.com, A Division of OldTimePatterns.com civilwarindex.com/armypa/185th_pa_regiment.html

rout, losing 1,200 men along the way. This series of events left the path to the North unguarded to Chambersburg.

Thus, with a force of 3,000 cavalry troops, Gilmor's Confederates circled to Chambersburg, reaching it by 30 July. They demanded a ransom from the populace and having no means of paying the amount; he raised the town by fire — the first Union town in the War to be deliberately destroyed.

Gilmor, a known daring Confederate cavalry officer, who later served as post-war Baltimore City Police Commissioner and Mayor, had been captured at least twice and imprisoned by Union troops, first in April 1861, in Baltimore, for rioting when Massachusetts and Pennsylvania state militia units, en route to the Washington, D.C., were assaulted. Then again, in September 1862, surrounding the Battle of Antietam and Lee's first attempt to invade the North — he was prisoner-exchanged both times. During Lee's second attempt to invade the North, at Gettysburg, he was commander of the First Maryland Cavalry and provost marshal of that town during its occupation. But he was more notoriously known for the Burning of Chambersburg, 30 July 1864, with his new command of Second Maryland Cavalry. Falsely reported arrested and killed by a "... a party of citizens, and literally trampled to death."[301] It proved untrue. "The rebel Major Harry Gilmor who was reported killed at Chambersburg, is alive and well, and was at Shepherdstown yesterday morning, with a small detachment of his command."[302]

Gilmor exclaimed: "The burning of Chambersburg was an awful sight, nor could I look on without deep sorrow, although I had become hardened by such scenes in Virginia."[303]

Undoubtedly the burning boiled the blood of Union calvary, many from the raised south-central Pennsylvania counties, leading up to the battle of Opequon in Winchester, 19 September 1864. Anthony's unit was fiercely involved with a *Harper's* magazine reporter writing: "These magnificent horsemen had then pressed up, sweeping before them the Confederate cavalry, and circling to the Confederate flank and rear. They charged fiercely upon the disorganized mass, which broke and fled in confusion to Winchester."[304]

---

[301] "Further From Chambersburg," *Baltimore Sun*, Baltimore, Maryland, 3 August 1864, page 1.

[302] *Baltimore Sun*, 4 August 1864, page 1.

[303] Gilmor, Col. Harry. *Four Years in the Saddle*. New York: Harper & Brothers, Publishers, 1866, page 212.

[304] *Harper's Pictorial History of the Civil War*. New York: Fairfax Press, 1866, page 710.

Harry Ward Gilmor (1838-1883)
Photograph by Matthew Brady, National Archives.

Historians believe these Union cavalrymen fought hard due to the wanton destruction of Chambersburg.

Effectively dispatching the Confederate cavalry, the Union units moved down the Luray Valley of Virginia pillaging and burning everything in sight. Anthony was promoted to Sergeant either before, but most likely, after this action on 19 September 1864. The event marked another turning point in the Shenandoah Valley in favor of the North. Confederate General Jubal Early's army, for the most part, remained intact but suffered further defeats at Fisher's Hill and Tom's Brook. Exactly a month later, the Valley Campaigns came to a close after Early's defeat at the Battle of Cedar Creek, Virginia.

On 15 October 1864, the horsemen were posted at Cedar Creek. A surprise attack on the 19th from the Confederate forces nearly defeated the Union encampment, but in the end was a clear victory, in which Anthony saw much action. A few days later on 23 October 1864, his unit was at Dry Run, but later moved back to Martinsburg, and remained there until 20 December, with the Union forces securely in control of the Shenandoah. The unit didn't see much action thereafter except minor skirmishes and scouting in the hills of West Virginia.

Sometime in January/February of 1865, Anthony may have gone on leave, as he was charged $4.50 for transportation at government expense. Not much more is known. His Company "L" consolidated into a newly formed Company "L" 3rd Regiment Pennsylvania Provincial Cavalry, created from the old Companies of "L" and a detachment of "H" of the 22nd, occurring 5 July 1865. He was listed absent during the July/August 1865 rolls, but we know they were in Greencastle, Pennsylvania, at the time. In September, he was on duty with his regular unit at "Post Comsy Mth Detc" — or detached service at the Commissary at Chambersburg.

On 31 October 1865, he was honorably discharged and mustered out at Cumberland, Maryland. They paid him $6.38 for clothing and a total of $300 bounty pay. He finally returned to Adams County to his family and farm. The regiment had 33 men killed in action, and 97 died from diseases.

THE SWORD

Anthony's cavalry sword is now preserved by the author, in Harrisburg, Pennsylvania. He probably wouldn't have used the sword as dismounted cavalry, and the sword would have been little use to him (if anything, it would have gotten in the way). The sword was produced for the United States cavalry in 1840 and issued as the US Model 1840 Heavy Cavalry saber, for enlisted men (not ornate like the officer issue).

"The model 1840 saber, called the 'wrist breaker,' [because it] was a relatively heavy cavalry saber, and as it was manufactured before the Civil War, it saw extensive use by both sides during the war mostly in parades. Standard features include a relatively straight wooden handle covered with leather and a wire grip, brass hilt has three branches, brass pommel cap and guard are unadorned, steel blade has flat back with narrow and wide fuller stopped at the ricasso, iron scabbard with iron mountings, throat is brazed and does not contain rivets. Manufactured by [William H.] Horstmann & Sons, and was actually assembled from mostly Prussian parts, and failed to gain acceptance by the government apparently because of this. Swords were sold to state and local militia units, and were not Federal inspected."[305]

"The brothers, Sigmund and William Horstmann, the successors of the founder, died within two years of each other, the former in 1870 and the latter in 1872. The business is continued under the same name, and no material changes have taken place. The house is recognized as the leading establishment in their special line in the United States."[306]

Anthony had relatives who joined in the War before his enlistment:

- Brother-in-law Thomas James Jefferson Stoops (1831-1894), a wagoner in Company C, 165th Pennsylvania Drafted Infantry Regiment; he was married to Anthony's sister, Ann Elizabeth (1830-1917).
- Brother James Stephen Sanders (1831-1895) served in Company C of the 165th and later in Company C of the 99th Pennsylvania Drafted Militia Infantry Regiment. He saw action at the end of the War at Petersburg.
- Brother Joseph Edmund Sanders (1838-1918) registered for the Draft but never served.[307]
- His brother John Jeremiah Sanders (1840-1909) was the first to sign-up from his family at first call for service 15 April 1861, but came down with typhoid fever the first month and was discharged. He lawfully registered for the Draft of June 1863, from Conewago Township, Adams County, 16th Congressional District; age 23, white, Farmer, Single, born in Pennsylvania. Undaunted, and recovered from his illness, he joined Company I, 26th Pennsylvania Militia "Emergency 1863" Infantry Regiment, June 1863. With spirited patriotism,

"The clashes of the untrained militiamen with Jubal Early's veteran rebels west and north of Gettysburg turned out as badly as could be expected. Several Pennsylvanians were shot and more

---

[305] Thillmann, John H., *Civil War Cavalry & Artillery Sabers,* Andrew Mowbray Publishers, 2001, page 215; also see Ridgeway, Harry. Civil War Relicman. www.relicman.com

[306] Robson, Charles. *Manufactories & Manufacturers of Pennsylvania of the Nineteenth Century.* Galaxy Publishing Company, 1875, pages 406-408, "Willliam H. Horstmann & Sons, Manufacturers of Dress Trimmings and Military Goods. 5th & Cherry Streets, Philadelphia, PA." www.workshopoftheworld.com/center_city/horstmann.html

[307] June 1863 Draft Registration, 16th Congressional District, age 24, white, Laborer, married, born in Pennsylvania. Volume 2 of 4.

James Stephen Sanders
Photograph from Brian Lee Cullison collection.

than a hundred rounded up as prisoners. The latter were paroled..."[308]

He was mustered out on 31 July 1863, listed as missing. But later, he showed up for honorable discharge in Harrisburg, 10 September. He

---

[308] gettysburg.stonesentinels.com/union-monuments/pennsylvania/penn-sylvania-infantry/26th-emergency-militia/

enlisted again in March 1864, apparently with the same unit. His post-war life is vague despite pension records. He ended up in Atlanta, Georgia by 1893, and died alone in a private sanatorium in 1909.

- Brother William Aloysious Sanders (1844-1915), was also a veteran of Company C, 165th, and later Company A, 91st Pennsylvania Volunteer Infantry Regiment. He saw much action in Virginia and was in the near vicinity of Appomattox Courthouse when Robert E. Lee surrendered.

POST-WAR

Post-war was kinder to Sergeant Anthony Sanders. He still didn't own land and remained a "farmhand" in the 1870 Census on the farm of his father-in-law.[309] But at least, he had a farmhouse with his wife and six children. However, in the house with his brother-in-law John Alexander Dick (1842-1931), also a veteran of the 22nd Cavalry, Company L, with his wife and two small children, who resided with them, peace was a rare commodity. In the War, John served as a division ambulance driver from October 1864 to April 1865, after first discharged earlier due to illness.

In 1880, Anthony was still living next door to his father-in-law, with wife Mary and with all nine of their children, humbly calling himself a "laborer."[310]

In 1890, enumerated by the Special Census,[311] he, too, was affected by the economic depression of this time and shortly after that, on 21 July 1890, he filed for an Invalid Pension, claiming on partial disability from rheumatism and lumbago. The affidavit witnesses were his sons, George Edward and Harvey Francis, both of Fairfield. It was sworn out by William H. Low,[312] Justice-of-the-Peace, and verified by John H. Stahle,[313] the Court Clerk. On 16 April 1891, he filed another affidavit before Justice Low. It was a busy month for Anthony; he was elected Surgeon, GAR Post James Dixon number 83.[314]

---

[309] 1870 U.S. Census, Hamiltonban Township, Adams County, Pennsylvania, NARA M593; Roll 1289; Page 180A.

[310] 1880 U.S. Census, Ibid., NARA T9; Roll 1085; Page: 29; Enumeration District 54.

[311] 1890 U.S. Special Census Schedule. Enumeration District 13, Hamiltonban Township, Adams County, Pennsylvania.

[312] A veteran and second lieutenant, Company C, 165th Regiment, Pennsylvania Drafted Militia.

[313] Stahle registered for the June 1863 Draft, but apparently never served.

[314] *Gettysburg Star & Sentinel*, 28 April 1891, page 3.

A November 1896 iota: "Mary Sanders is reported ill," but she recovered.[315]

"Mr. and Mrs. Anthony Sanders, of near Iron Springs, gave an enjoyable reception Wednesday of last week, in honor of the marriage of their daughter, Mary, to Mr. James Peters, of near Waynesboro. The dinner was [a] fine one, the table being ladened with all the good things of the season. Those present were: James Peters and bride, John Peters, wife and two children, George Peters, Grace Sanders, Geo. Sanders and three children, James Sanders, Harvy [sic] Sanders, Chas. Wachter, Maggie Burns, John Dick, wife and two sons, Hill Sanders, Clarence Sanders, Oliver McCleaf, Maggie McCleaf, Henry Herring, David Finefrock and wife, Benj. Coll, John Hoffman and wife, Regina Peters."[316]

On 4 July 1898, he replied to a Bureau of Pensions questionnaire, having received a pension at the time.

Again, on 17 February 1900, he filed for the upgrading of his pension and stated his residence as being in Iron Springs. Yet that year on 17 April, he swore out a General Affidavit affirming no post-military service.

May 1900: Still the horseman, Anthony was the Grand Marshall escort with the visit of Bishop Shanahan to administer the sacrament of Confirmation upon a class. "...to see those sturdy farmers riding their prancing horses with ease and grace..." was an event for Catholics and non-Catholics alike in a little town of 400 souls.[317]

The June 1900 U.S. Census has the aging couple (66 and 64 years) finally owning their own home and with Anthony describing himself as a day laborer.[318] Sons Edward Charles and Henry Leo and niece Virginia L. Peters were living with them.

The gossipy newspapers reported the Civil War veterans' family activities:

September 1902: "Iron Springs, Sept. 19. — Mr. Anthony Sanders and wife have returned home from an extended trip to Chambersburg."[319]

---

[315] "Fountain Dale Items," *Adams County Independent,* 14 November 1896, page 1.

[316] *Adams County Independent*, 26 February 1898, page 1.

[317] Ibid., 16 June 1900, page 3.

[318] NARA T623; Roll 1354; Page 4A; Page 210; Line 49-50; Enumeration District 18; Hamiltonban Township, Adams County, Pennsylvania.

[319] *Adams County Independent*, 20 September 1902, page 1.

June 1903: "Mrs. A. G. Sanders was called to Chambersburg to see her grandchild, Leo Peters, son of James Peters, who is lying ill with typhoid fever."[320] By July 3, she was still at the house.[321]

September 1903: "Mrs. Marietta Sanders, daughter of Frederick Shulley, and little boy, from Chambersburg, were the guests of her father-in-law Anthony Sanders and family last Saturday."[322] [323]

December 1903: "Anthony Sanders and wife who were helping their son-in-law James Peters and family to move to Chambersburg returned home recently."[324] [325]

1904 was a mixed year for Anthony. Deaths of old comrades and accidents plagued him:
• January: Anthony was a Pallbearer for William Smith, a veteran of Company C, 165th Infantry.[326]
• February: "Anthony Sanders while cutting wood one day last week, inflicted a gash in his lower limb which we are glad to report is not serious."[327] [328]
• June: he filed for a Declaration for Invalid Pension, as required. Next month, 4 July, he filed for another Invalid Pension, claiming on age, rheumatism, lumbago, heart trouble, and dyspepsia. It was witnessed by J. M. Musselman and J. H. Creager.
• November: He again was a Pallbearer for Robert [Francis] Watson, a Civil War veteran of Company B, 190th Regiment, Pennsylvania Volunteer Infantry, a cousin of Frederick M. Shulley and neighbor.[329]
• November: "Mr. Anthony Sanders recently met with quite a painful accident by cutting a deep gash in his foot."[330] [331]

THE END IS AT HAND BY 1905

---

320 Ibid., 27 June 1903, page 5.
321 Ibid., 4 July 1903, page 1.
322 *Gettysburg Compiler*, 9 September 1903, page 2.
323 *Adams County Independent*, 12 September 1903, page 5.
324 Ibid., 12 December 1903, page 1.
325 *Gettysburg Compiler*, 23 December 1903, page 2.
326 Ibid., 13 January 1904, page 2.
327 Ibid., 17 February 1904, page 2.
328 *Adams County Independent*, 13 February 1904, page 4.
329 *Gettysburg Compiler*, 2 November 1904, page 10.
330 Ibid., 30 November 1904, page 8.
331 *Adams County Independent*, 16 November 1904, page 8.

Father Time, by now, was counting the clock for both Anthony and Mary — both now in their 70s.

• February: "Mr. Anthony Sanders is reported on the sick list."[332] "...a member of the G. A. R. Post..."[333]

• March: "Anthony Sanders who had been confined to his home, is able to be out again."[334] [335]

• And by April Anthony was feeling his oats and was elected delegate from Hamiltonban Township to the Republican convention at Gettysburg, 17 April 1905.[336] And, "Mr. A. G. Sanders is improving his property by putting a new roof on the out-kitchen."[337]

• August: "Mrs. Anthony Sanders a highly respected lady is very ill at this time. Dr. Glenn is the attending physician."[338]

• September: "Mrs. A. G. Sanders, of near this place, is very ill at this time. The family has telegraphed to their son, John Sanders, who went West 20 years ago, to come home at once."[339]

"John Sanders, formerly from this place, who has been living in Des Moines, Iowa, for over 22 years arrived here on Friday night, the first to see his aged mother, Mrs. Anthony Sanders, who has been very ill for sometime. Edward Sanders and wife from Bonneauville, Wm. Sanders and wife from near Emmitsburg, Md., were at home.

On last Sunday morning, Sept 3, death visited the community by taking Mrs. Anthony Sanders, whose maiden name was Mary Dick, after an illness of about 2 weeks, aged 70 years, 2 months and 27 days. She is survived by her husband, Anthony Sanders, two brothers, John Dick Sr. of this place and Geo Dick of Chambersburg, one sister, Hester Fitzgerald of Baltimore, Md., and the following children: Peter J. and Harvey F. Sanders of Chambersburg, Harriet S. Hoffman and James S. Sanders of Fairfield, John E. Sanders of Des Moines, Mary M. Peters of near Chambersburg, Geo. E. Sanders of near Fairfield, Henry L. Sanders of this place, Edward C. Sanders of Gettysburg. She was born at this place and living here all her life. Mrs. Sanders is considered by every one who knew her to have been especially kind to her neighbors in sickness, ready to lend

---

332 Ibid., 18 February 1905, page 4.

333 Ibid., 25 February 1905, page 4.

334 Ibid., 11 March 1905, page 4.

335 *Gettysburg Compiler,* 15 March 1905, page 3.

336 *Adams County Independent*, 29 April 1905, page 1.

337 "Chronicle of Events From Iron Springs," *Adams County Independent*, 29 April 1905, page 1.

338 *Gettysburg Compiler*, 30 August 1905, page 8.

339 *Adams County Independent,* 2 September 1905, page 5.

a helping hand to any one in need and will be missed in the community in which she has lived so long. Funeral services will be held in the Fairfield Catholic church on Tues. morning, September 5th at 10 o'clock a.m., to which church deceased belonged all her life, attending all services of her church, traveling through rain and over muddy roads never missing unless prevented by sickness. Interment will take place in the Catholic cemetery of Fairfield."[340] [341]

Shortly after Mary's death, Anthony packed up his worldly possessions and moved in with daughter Harriet and son-in-law John Hoffman in Fairfield, who had no children and had the space.[342] Earlier, he had a well-attended sale of his belonging in Iron Springs.[343] A few days later, "Mr. John Dick, Jr., moved into the house of Anthony Sanders last Thursday. Mr. Sanders expects to make his home with John Hoffman, of Fairfield."[344]

In June 1907, he received a pension, under the new Act of 1907, of $15 per month.[345]

Later, in November, "Anthony Sanders, an aged Civil War veteran, is on the sick list."[346]

In April 1908, he sold his house to his son Harry Leo.[347] That September, Anthony became a small-town hero when he gave the alarm that saved the town of Fairfield from a fire started in the barn of his son James Sanders spreading to five other barns. It could have been a catastrophe if not for the quick actions of the towns citizens.[348] In December, widower Anthony filed for another pension under the "Act of February 6, 1907." He gave his address as Fairfield. The affidavit witnessed by Henry D. Peters, of Iron Springs, and Thadeus S. T. Stultz of Fairfield, and sworn before Justice-of-

---

[340] *Gettysburg Compiler,* 6 September 1905, page 8.

[341] *Valley Spirit,* 13 September 1905, page 3.

[342] "Chronicle of Events From Iron Springs," *Adams County Independent,* 30 September 1905, page 1.

[343] *Gettysburg Compiler,* 4 October 1905, page 2.

[344] *Adams County Independent,* 7 October 1905, page 4. John Albert Dick, Jr. was the son of John Alexander Dick, brother-in-law of Anthony.

[345] *New Oxford Item,* 6 June 1907, page 5. *Adams County Independent,* 6 June 1907, page 3. *York Dispatch,* newspaper, York, York County, Pennsylvania. 1 June 1907, page 2.

[346] *Adams County Independent,* 23 November 1907, page 4.

[347] "News Items from Jack's Mountain," *Adams County Independent,* 11 April 1908, page 1.

[348] *Adams County Independent,* 19 September 1908, page 1. New Oxford Item, 24 September 1908, page 5.

the-Peace William H. Low, all veterans of Company C, 165th Regiment.

In August 1909 he made local newspaper headlines:

"Anthony Sanders Taken Suddenly Ill While Visiting In Emmitsburg.

Anthony G. Sanders, an aged veteran of the Civil War, while visiting friends at Emmitsburg, last week, was taken suddenly ill, and went at once to a Baltimore hospital where he is under going treatment at this time. He was visited at the hospital by his daughter, Mrs. John Hoffman, and his son, James Sanders, who found him somewhat improved.[349]

But two months later in October: Dr. Trout has taken Anthony Sanders back to the hospital in Baltimore where he had an operation performed. It is feared his contracting blood poisening."[350] [351]

Anthony lingered and declined for another two years, and on 26 October 1911:

"Anthony G. Sanders Dies at the Home of his Daughter in Fairfield. ...

Anthony G. Sanders died at the home of his daughter, Mrs. Hoffman in Fairfield, Thursday evening about 5 o'clock from a complication of diseases at the age of 77 years, 11 months and 22 days.

He was a Civil War veteran having serviced in Co. L, 22nd Cavalry, and a member of James Dixon Post G. A. R. No. 83.

He is survived by the following children, Peter and Harvey Sanders, and Mrs. Mary Peters, of Chambersburg; George E. and Harry L. Sanders and Mrs. Harriett Hoffman, of Fairfield; John Elmer Sanders, of Des Moines, Iowa; James S. and Edward Sanders, of Gettysburg. He is also survived by two brother, William Sanders, of Edge Grove and Edward Sanders of Mt. Rock, and two sisters, Mrs. Sarah Hoffman, of Fairfield and Mrs. Elizabeth Grothe, of York.

Funeral Saturday morning with services in the Catholic church at 10 o'clock. Rev. John Connaghan officiating. Interment in Catholic cemetery."[352,353]

At the time of his death, Anthony was receiving a $20 per month pension, and on 2 March 1912, he was officially dropped from pension rolls.

Anthony and Mary left a legacy of good works and over 1,000 descendants known at the time of this essay.

---

[349] Ibid., 21 August 1909, page 1.

[350] *Gettysburg Times,* 29 October 1909, page 1.

[351] *Adams County News*, 30 October 1909, page 4.

[352] *Gettysburg Times,* 27 October 1911; page 1.

[353] *Adams County News*, 28 October 1911, page 8.

FAIRFIELD

Fairfield. May 31—The memorial services in the Reformed church last Sunday afternoon were largely attended. The sermon was preached by Rev. Charles Dalzell, of Presbyterian church. Music was furnished by the church choir. The following veterans of the Civil War were present, P. H. Riley, John Manberz, William H. Baker, William W. Paddock, Adam Snyder, George F. Sites, John C. Sites, John C. Moore, Emanuel E. King, William H. Kentzel, Samuel Walter, Peter S. Harbaugh, Joseph H. Creager, Charles F. Hoffman, Henry J. Beard, John F. Wetzel and John Dubbs The following members of the G. A. R post of Fairfield died since decoration day 1911, Frederick Shulley, who served in Co. G. 209th Regiment Pennsylvaina Volunteers, died August 12, 1911; Anthony G. Sanders who served in Co. K. 22nd Cavalry, died October 28th, 1911.

Adams County News, *Gettysburg, Pennsylvania. 1 June 1912, page 4.*

Library of Congress.

VI. The Substitute

We're coming, ancient Abraham, several hundred strong,
We hadn't no 300 dollars so we came along
We hadn't no parents pony up the tin
So we went unto the provost and there were mustered in. —
    Carl Sandburg, *Abraham Lincoln, The War Years*[354]

---

[354] Volume 2, page 155. New York: Harcourt Brace and Company, 1939. A ditty attributed to Irish-American draftees of the Civil War.

There is a part of American Civil War history that stirs up much controversy in civilian life — from the Revolutionary War to the Vietnam War — forced military conscription.

With the war effort by the Union failing in the first years and volunteers drying up, the new draft law, the Enrollment Act of 3 March 1863,[355] required registration of every male citizen, including immigrants filing for citizenship between ages 25-45. Men mentally or physically impaired, the only son of a widow, or infirm parents or a widower with dependent children, were exempt. Establishing quotas for each congressional district, the draftee could have another individual go in his stead. It was also the option of a draftee to pay a commutation fee of $300 — or just over $6,000 in today's terms[356] — for someone to take his place. In 1863, it was a princely sum, and lead to the "rich-man's battle but a poor man's war" complaint and violent riots. Indeed, New York City experienced a riot with 120 protesters killed and 2,000 injured a few months after the implementation of the Draft.[357]

Men looking for the exemption come before the local Board receipt-in-hand paid to the Collector of Internal Revenue or with the name of the substitute.

Reasons for evasion of the Draft, other than previously cited, were broad: religious pacifism, fear of death, fear of military life which was pretty rough and disease-laden, having a young family, business activities, opposition to the War for political reasons, or other family members having already served, and so forth.

Despite the avoidance of service conotation, a Substitute was reasonably common in the era; even future President Grover Cleveland paid a $300 commutation fee.

Although the War was also particularly unpopular everywhere, many just accepted the Draft predicament forced upon them and believed the War would end soon anyway. With the implementation of the Draft, by the end of 1864, the ranks of the Union Army swelled from 576,000 to 918,000 troops and helped conclude the conflict.[358]

---

[355] §12 Stat. 731, Public Law 37-75.

[356] Bureau of Labor Statistics consumer price index calculation. However, using labor value, it could well be over $50,000 in today's context.

[357] Williams, Keith. "Did Firefighters Start or End 1863 Draft Riots — or Both?" *New York Times,* 23 July 2017, Section MB, Page 3.

[358] Shannon, Fred Albert *The Organization and Administration of the Union Army, 1861-1865.* Volumes 1 and 2. Cleveland, Ohio: The Arthur H. Clark Company, 1928.

William Myers Doner, a 28-year-old married farmer, dutifully registered for the Draft in June 1863 from the 15th Congressional District, in Cumberland County, Pennsylvania. William, conscripted into Company G, 26th Pennsylvania Emergency Militia as a Private, but "... procured a substitute for 9 Months."[359] It is unknown who was his substitute, and he did not serve later during the War. William could afford the substitution, coming from a long line of well-established wealthy farmers in what is Lancaster, Lebanon, and Cumberland counties.

Born 4 January 1835 on the family farm, in North Middleton Township, Cumberland County, son of John Doner and Anna Myers, he acquired his middle name from his mother's maiden surname.[360]

William was a descendant of Michael Doner (1690-1762)[361] and wife Magdalena Landis (1692-1789)[362], immigrants allegedly from a German-speaking Canton in Switzerland, arriving "...about 1717 and purchased on February 20, 1718 from George Doner[363] and Barbara Kendrick of the London Company 200 acres..." On Au-

---

[359] NARA M554 Roll 30. However, the NARA and Pennsylvania State Archives do not have any evidence of his conscientious objections from official lists. Transcribed and compiled by volunteers of the Genealogical Society of Pennsylvania from entries in the 'Register of Aliens & Persons Having Conscientious Scruples Against Bearing Arms, 1862,' (entry #3168); Records of State and District Offices, 1861-72, Pennsylvania (Part IV), Western Division; Records of the Provost Marshal General's Bureau, Record Group 110; National Archives Building, Washington, DC.

[360] Middle name: family Bible pages in possession of the author. Internet media mistakenly has "Mathias" taken from the death certificate of his daughter Laura Belle Doner Clay (1867-1942). The informant for the record was Dr. Anita Wilson Harper, a psychiatrist at the Harrisburg State Hospital who had little knowledge of the family, and used the name of Laura's father-in-law, Mathias Clay. The confusion was compounded when Laura's husband, Jacob Henry Clay (1866-1942), died eight days earlier from prostrate cancer. Laura died of heart disease, but was previously committed to the hospital for psychosis. It is unknown why their grieved three sons were unaware of the mistake.

[361] Variations of the surname: Dohner, Doner, Donner, Dorner, Downer, etc.

[362] Her surname is according to *Mennonite Vital Records*. Lancaster Mennonite Historical Society. Lancaster, Lancaster County, Pennsylvania. www.lmhs.org

[363] Relationship unknown.

```
┌─────────────────────────────────────┐
│   Michael Doner - Magdalena Landis   │
│    1690-1762           1692-1789     │
└─────────────────────────────────────┘
                  │
                  ▼
┌─────────────────────────────────────┐
│  Abraham Doner - Magdalena Landis    │
│    1732-1787           1744-1794     │
└─────────────────────────────────────┘
                  │
                  ▼
┌─────────────────────────────────────┐
│  Daniel Doner - Elizabeth Musser     │
│    1781-1853           1779-1875     │
└─────────────────────────────────────┘
                  │
                  ▼
┌─────────────────────────────────────┐
│    John Doner - Anna Myers           │
│    1808-1895       1815-1891         │
└─────────────────────────────────────┘
                  │
                  ▼
┌─────────────────────────────────────┐
│ William Myers DONER - Mary Ann Kiehl │
│   1835-1910              1839-1899    │
└─────────────────────────────────────┘
```

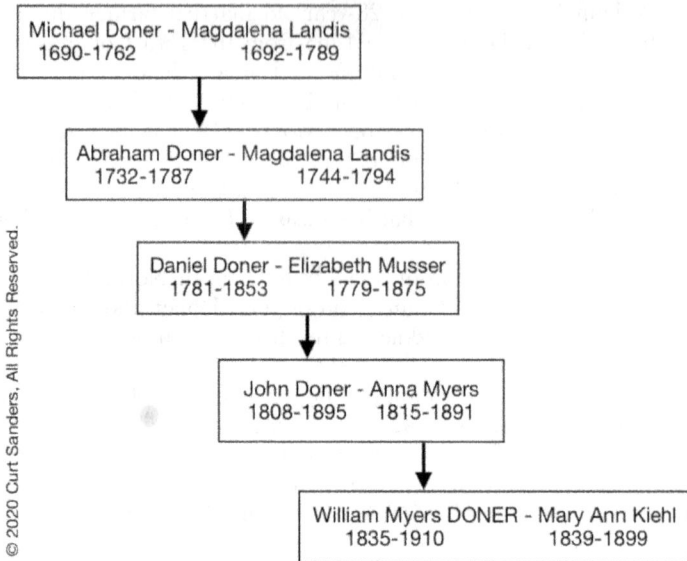

gust 22, 1734 he purchased [an additional] 260 acres…"[364] So started a wealthy dynasty of Mennonite farmers, that by the 1860s, for this line of progeny, transformed into Lutheran communicants.

William's reluctance to join the military is unknown nor noted in the sparse draft ledger.[365] His native county had its share of Copperheads,[366] but the influential local *Carlisle Weekly Herald* newspaper was virulently pro-Union and made every effort to unbraid "traitors" and like persons within its pages.

But, by the end of the War, he and his wife Mary Ann *nee* Kiehl (1839-1899) were solid members at Saint Matthew's Evangelical Lutheran Church, Plainfield, so we can safely dismiss any lingering Mennonite pacifism. He already had three small children by wife

---

[364] Landis, Ira D. "The Earliest Doner Family in America," *Mennonite Research Journal,* Lancaster Mennonite Historical Society. XVIII April, 1977, No. 2.

[365] NARA M554 roll 30; Record Group 110; entry 172; MN-65.

[366] A Peace Democrat opposed to federal military intervention of the succession states. They earned the name "Copperhead" from their use of a penny lapel pin.

Mary Ann, whom he married 16 September 1858 in Cumberland County.[367]

The children were:

i.   Amanda Alice "Jennie" Doner (born three months after her parent's marriage, 1859-1939), later married first Jacob T. Brehm and then Alfred Shearer.

ii. Mary Magdalene Doner (1861-1942); married Wilson W. Ensminger.

iii. And the fragile Frances Ann Doner (1862—who died after William's draft registration, 1863).

His brother, Emanuel David Doner (1841-1915) was called-up into Company "C" 158th Regiment Drafted Militia of Pennsylvania, on 16 October 1862. The unit organized at Chambersburg in November and ordered to Suffolk, Virginia, where it remained until 28 December 1862, when they moved to New Berne, North Carolina, with the 1st Brigade 5th Division, 18th Corps. The unit became involved in the expeditions from New Berne to Trenton, Pollocksville, Young's Crossroads and Swansborough, North Carolina, 6-10 March 1863, and again from New Berne to Washington, North Carolina on 7 Apr 1863. Two days later, the unit moved out to Kinston, North Carolina, and saw action on the 19th at Big Swift Creek. In June 1863, they went to Fortress Monroe, Virginia. Emanuel's unit missed the Battle of Gettysburg but moved to Harper's Ferry by 7-9 July to block the retreat of the Confederates coming back from Gettysburg. The regiment engaged in this pursuit for about three weeks, and by 24 July, it reported to Boonesboro, Maryland. His nine-month enlistment contract expired, so he was discharged shortly after that.[368]

Emanuel reenlisted with his brother, Samuel Alexander Doner (1843-1878), in Company F, 207th Pennsylvania Volunteer Infantry, in August 1864 and marched off to Washington, D. C. for training. A short few weeks later, thrown into the siege operations against Petersburg and Richmond. Seeing action 5-7 February 1865 at the Battle of Dobney's Mills, Hatcher's Run, Armstrong Mills, Rowanty Creek's, and Vaughn Road, in Virginia. Over a month later, on 25 March 1865, the unit was involved in the calamitous, but a triumphant assault on Ft. Steadman, Virginia. On 2 April 1865, the regiment was part of the primary attack on the Confederates lines at Petersburg, in which Samuel was wounded. Emanuel was at the 15 April 1865 Appomattox Courthouse surrender of Confederate forces

---

[367] *American Volunteer,* newspaper, Carlisle, Cumberland County, Pennsylvania; 23 September 1858.

[368] Dyer, page 1620.

under Robert E. Lee, marking the *de facto* end of the War. They, with their unit, were officially mustered-out, 31 May 1865.[369]

Brother-in-law, David Cully (1839-1905), married to their sister Barbara Ann Doner (1845-1923), also draft registered but did not serve.[370] The rest of the family were too young.

William kept a low profile throughout his life. He was content working on his farm. No newspaper accounts rebuked him for his substitute service, but the post-war culture was less-than-kind to others.

In the 1880 Census, they were raising a family and enjoying the fruits of their labors in Dickinson Township, Cumberland County.[371]

He and Mary Ann produced six more children:

iv. Calvin Elsworth Doner (1864-1940), later married to Caroline Elmira Wise.
v.   Elmer Lincoln Doner (1865-1958); married Ella Kutz.
vi. Laura Bell Doner (1867-1942); married Jacob Henry Clay.
vii. Ida Jane Doner (1873-1935); married Bertus Eberly Davis, son of William Henry Davis previously mentioned in chapter one.
viii. Flora Ellen "Ella" Doner (1874-1934); married Curtis M. Reitzel.
ix. Carrie Ettie Doner (1879-1883).

Age was creeping up on William. So, in March 1884, he slowly dissolved his farm by selling off five workhorses, 24 bred cattle, sheep, hogs, and farming implements.[372]

Insolvent by November 1890, he sold the "Limestone Farm," of seventy acres, with house and barn, orchard, well and tract of woodland, to William H. Leppert in October 1890.[373]

William and Mary were living on Reservoir Hill, Chambersburg, when she passed away, the day before Christmas, 1899.[374]

Wife Mary Ann *nee* Kiehl was a daughter of another Pennsylvania "Dutch" family prominent in Cumberland County history. Her

---

[369] Dyer, page 1625.

[370] Draft Registration, 15th Congressional District, June 1863, age 24, white, Laborer, unmarried, born in Pennsylvania.

[371] NARA T9; Sheet 346D; Enumeration District 82; Line 31-32.

[372] *The Sentinel,* Carlisle, Cumberland County, Pennsylvania, 28 January 1884, page 3; notice of coming sale.

[373] *Carlisle Weekly Herald,* 30 October 190, page 3.

[374] *Harrisburg Telegraph,* 28 December 1899, page 2; 29 December 1899, page 3; *Public Opinion,* 26 December 1899, page 3; 27 December 1899, page 4; 29 December 1899, page 8; *People's Register,* 29 December 1899, page 1; *Valley Spirit,* 27 December 1899, page 5; *Carlisle Evening Herald*, 26 December 1899, page 4; *Carlisle Evening Sentinel,* 27 December 1899, page 3.

father, Abraham J. Kiehl (ca1810-1891), was a farmer first married to Frances __?__ (1813-1860), her mother.

Mary's life and family was upended when her brother, John F. Kiehl (1843-1899) was charged with the murder of his wife, Sarah Elizabeth Doner (born 1839), in May 1871. Sarah was the sister to William Myers Doner. She died an egregious death by poison after a few days of lingering torture. Because of the nature of her death, the authorities summoned enough evidence to arrest him; banking on the mode of death and the rocky relationship between the two, witnessed by neighbors and relatives.

The trial turned-out a sensation that was widely cited in national newspapers. Nevertheless, John was acquitted and he remarried and removed to Lancaster County. But it divided the family since William and others testified against John.[375,376] The trial later became an example case for the Harvard Law School.

Oddly, nothing can be found of William in the following 1900 and 1910 Censuses — not even living with his children. But we know by his death certificate, 30 September 1910, he was living in Frankford Township and buried with his wife in Chambersburg.[377] Despite his wife's copious death notices, no newspaper obituary is found of him other than a grudgingly "Mrs. Annie Cully and two daughters attended the funeral of the former's brother, William Doner, held in Chambersburg on Monday."[378]

But the Doner's receded into the quiet farm life and can proudly be remembered with an abundance of descendants throughout the United States of America. William is remembered by supplying his country with the goods and services to keep it going.

---

[375] "The Kiehl Murder Trial," *Carlisle Herald*, 23 November 1871, pages 1, 2; 14 December 1871, pages 1, 2.

[376] *The Kiehl Murder Trial! The Trial of John Kiehl, for the Poisoning of His Wife Sarah E. Kiehl, On the 7th Day of May 1871.* Carlisle, Pennsylvania: Herald Office, 1871. A book about the trial.

[377] Death certificate, Commonwealth of Pennsylvania, file number 536.

[378] *Valley Times-Star*, Newville, Cumberland County, Pennsylvania, 6 October 1910, page 8.

A pensitive President Abraham Lincoln allegedly before signing the Emancipation proclamation. — *U.S.Army War College archives.*

VII. A subject of Importance.

D espite this multi-essay focusing on the American Civil War and the Gilded Age, it barely touches upon the attitude of its subjects toward an issue of the War: slavery. The essays were mined details about their lives during and after the War with factual information.

Our subject's pension records were void of political partiality and were examples of rout nineteenth-century bureaucrat-speak. The newspapers would include opinions and pronouncements on various topics but not from our featured soldiers. Since we have no surviving letters from them, one can only guess what they thought of slavery.

Twenty-first-century readers of copious history books suggest that slavery was a central issue of the War. It was too many. Witness: John Brown's Raid, Bloody Kansas, many active abolitionist societies, and celebrities, indeed, are at the forefront of people's minds.

The Confederacy, in part, based its separatist act upon the expansion of slavery and the preservation of that institution. In a review of the local northern newspapers of the age, slavery was not a hot topic except in the editorial columns. Only after the Emancipation Proclamation of 1 January 1863, freeing under federal law, more than three million enslaved human beings were in the Confederate states. It pushed slavery even further to the front into political and social interest. Even then, it was more complex for the northern soldier, farmer, and worker. The exception was usually the (Irish) immigrant who faced perceived increased competition for jobs flooding the north because of the decree. Witness the infamous "Draft Riots" in Lower Manhattan. The issue of slavery may have caused moral outrage, but it was off to a distant "foreign" land for most.

For the everyday poor white person in the Confederacy, the issue was an invasion of foreigners — a group of states set upon another. For the white person residing in the federal Union, it was a mix:

- Preservation of the Union; putting down an illegal rebellion
- Quick bonus cash for a year's service
- A class fight between interests controlling the North and the South
- Preventing the spread of slavery — probably in that order or something like it.

Like most northern soldiers, the book subjects joined military service for various reasons. A $300 enlistment bounty was astronomically beautiful when the nation's economic growth was stagnant and deficient. Also, their neighbors, friends, and relatives joined up, making the peer pressure intense, especially in the southern tier state counties suffering from rebel raiders stealing or destroying their belongings. After the Draft law of March 1863, it was coercion by fiat from the local Provost Marshal.

Davis brought up in a family with deep martial roots and a long-preserved Union, hinted he joined for patriotic and financial reasons.

Shulley's record is silent on the question, but his abolitionist Company Orderly, Sgt. Wert reported that the "blacks were our only friends while in Virginia." Wert and the men of Company G were neighbors, relatives, and friends and probably shared similar views.

Like many in the area, Sanders came from a family who opposed the War or were non-committal. Still, self-interest and the intrusions from rebel raiders pushed them into the fray. The money was agreeable, too. They probably did not care about slavery — it was someone else's problem in another far off state.

Aldrich and Doner, going by their family religious histories, probably opposed slavery via lingering pacifist convictions and saw slavery as violence against fellow humans.

It is evident, by chronology, that most of our subjects joined the War effort when it was clear the Union was winning. Alternatively, with a threat of rebel forces charging back into their home front.

Living in south-central Pennsylvania, Davis, Shulley, Sanders, and Doner probably came in contact with a black person sometime in their life — and definitely while in military service in the South. They were well aware of the local newspapers advertising the return of runaway enslaved peoples and living only 5-30 miles from the Mason-Dixon Line that separated the free from the enslaved. The Christiana Resistance of 1851 still fresh in their minds.

Kilborn and Aldrich probably never met a person of color until they were in the military in Tennessee and Virginia, respectively.

Post-war political opinions by our essay subjects reveal nothing. Many joined a quasi-political fraternal organization, the Grand Army of the Republic, that advocated for black voting rights and veteran pensions. It supported like-minded candidates and monument dedications, but mostly, it was a local connection of vets for comradeship.

In sum, all had deep northern family roots in the seventeenth century and did not want to see a nation divided their ancestors had built.

Bibliography

1786 Pennsylvania Septennial Census, Washington Township, Franklin County, Pennsylvania.

1886 History of Adams County, Pennsylvania. (Originally published as *History of Cumberland and Adams Counties*). Chicago: Warner, Beers & Co., 1886 (reprinted, The Bookmark, Knightstown, Indiana, 1977).

Adams County Independent, newspaper, Littlestown, Adams County, Pennsylvania.

Adams County News, newspaper, Gettysburg, Adams County, Pennsylvania.

Adams Sentinel, newspaper, Gettysburg, Adams County, Pennsylvania.

American Volunteer, newspaper, Carlisle, Cumberland County, Pennsylvania.

Arrington, Benjamin T., "Industry and Economy during the Civil War," *National Park Service.* www.nps.gov/articles/industry-and-economy-during-the-civil-war.htm

Baltimore Sun, newspaper, Baltimore, Maryland.

Barrows, Isabel C., editor. National Conference of Charities and Correction, 24th Session, 1897.

Barton, Michael, Editor. *Glorious Recollections: J. Howard Wert's Lost History of the 209th Regiment, Pennsylvania Volunteer Infantry, 1864-1865, including the Defense of Bermuda Hundred, the Battle of Fort Stedman and the Storming of Petersburg, with Additional Document.* 2016.

Bates, Samuel Penniman. *History of Pennsylvania Volunteers, 1861-5; prepared in compliance with acts of the legislature.* Harrisburg, Pennsylvania: B. Singerly, State Printer, 1870.

Blanck, Peter. "Civil War Pensions and Disability," *Ohio State Law Journal,* Volume 62:109. (Blanck's narrative is definitive study of the pension era and process.)

Bloom, Robert L., Emeritus, Gettysburg College. "We Never Expected a Battle," *The Civilians at Gettysburg, 1863.* Gettysburg, Pennsylvania.

Brennan, John. *The Michigan Historical Marker Web Site.* www.mich-markers.com/default?page=L1844. January 2020.

Camp Curtin Historical Society, P.O. Box 5601, Harrisburg, Pennsylvania 17110. www.campcurtin.org

Carlisle Herald, newspaper, Carlisle, Cumberland County, Pennsylvania.

Carlisle Evening Herald, newspaper, Carlisle, Cumberland County, Pennsylvania.

Carlisle Weekly Sentinel, newspaper, Carlisle, Cumberland County, Pennsylvania.

Catalogue of Jefferson Medical College of Philadelphia Session of 1849-50. Philadelphia: Frick and Kelly, Printers, 1850.

CivilWarIndex.com, A Division of OldTimePatterns.com

Clark, Walter. *Histories of the Several Regiments and Battalions from North Carolina in the Great War 1861-'65.* Goldsboro, North Carolina: Nash Brothers, 1901.

Coldwater Sentinel, newspaper, Coldwater, Branch County, Michigan.

The Compiler, newspaper, Gettysburg, Adams County, Pennsylvania.

Courier Post, newspaper, Camden, New Jersey.

The Center for Disease Control, Atlanta, Georgia. "Achievements in Public Health, 1900-1999: Control of Infectious Diseases," *Morbidity and Mortality Weekly Report.*

Daily Telegraph, newspaper, Harrisburg, Dauphin County, Pennsylvania.

Dasef, John W. *History of Montcalm County, Michigan; Its People, Industries and Institutions.* Indianapolis, Indiana: B.F. Bowen & Company Inc., 1916.

Davis, Rev. Thomas Kirby. *The Davis Family Book, A History of the Descendants of William Davis and his Wife, Mary Means.* Norwood, Massachusetts: The Plimpton Press, 1912.

Davis, William Watts Hart. *A Genealogical and Personal History of Bucks County, Pennsylvania.* New York, 1905.

Defebaugh, James E. *History of The Lumber Industry of America.* Chicago: American Lumberman, 1907.

Democratic Advocate, newspaper, Westminster, Frederick County, Maryland.

Dictionary of American Family Names. Oxford University Press, 2003.

Dohner, Dudley Howard. *The Dohner Newsletter.* Various years.

Dyer, Frederick H. *A Compendium of the War of the Rebellion.* Des Moines, Iowa: 1908; reprinted 1979 The Press of Morningstar Bookshop, Dayton, Ohio.

Elwood, Sergeant John W. *Elwood's Stories of the Old Ringgold Cavalry 1847-1865.* Coal Center, Pennsylvania: Morgantown Printing and Binding Company, 1914.

Foote, Shelby. *The Civil War: A Narrative.* Volume 2, *Fredericksburg to Meridan.* New York: Random House, 1958.

Foreman, Amanda. *A World on Fire: An Epic History of Two Nations Divided.* London: Penguin, 2010.

Friends, Society of. *U. S. Encyclopedia of American Quaker Genealogy.* Volumes I - IV, 1607-1943. Library of Congress, 1910.

Frost, Josephine C.; Friends, Society of. *Quaker Records From Farmington Monthly Meeting, Ontario County, New York.* Library of Congress, 1910.

The Gazette, newspaper, York, York County, Pennsylvania.

Gettysburg Complier, newspaper, Gettysburg, Adams County, Pennsylvania.

Gettysburg Star & Sentinel, newspaper, Gettysburg, Adams County, Pennsylvania.

Gettysburg.stonesentinels.com

Gettysburg Times, newspaper, Gettysburg, Adams County, Pennsylvania.

Gillett, Mary C. *The Army Medical Department 1818-1865.* Washington, D.C: Center of Military History United States Army, 1987.

Gilmor, Col. Harry. *Four Years in the Saddle.* New York: Harper & Brothers, Publishers, 1866.

Gorman, Kathleen L."Civil War Pensions." Essential Civil War Curriculum, Virginia Center for Civil War Studies at Virginia Tech. May 2012. www.essentialcivilwarcurriculum.com/civil-war-pensions.html

Gragg, Rod. *The Illustrated Gettysburg Reader: An Eyewitness History of the Civil War's Greatest Battle.* Washington, DC: Regnery History.

Guelzo, Allen C. *Gettysburg: The Last Invasion.* New York: Vintage Civil War Library, Vintage Books, 2013.

Gustafson, A. M. *Douglass, A Michigan Township.* 1982.

Harper's Pictorial History of the Civil War. New York: Fairfax Press, 1866.

Harrisburg Daily Independent, newspaper, Harrisburg, Dauphin County, Pennsylvania.

Harrisburg Telegraph, newspaper, Harrisburg, Dauphin County, Pennsylvania.

Heth, Henry to J. Williams Jones, June 1877, *Southern Historical Society Papers;* reprint, Millwood, New York: 1977.

The Inquirer, newspaper, Lancaster, Lancaster County, Pennsylvania.

Intelligencer Journal, newspaper, Lancaster, Lancaster County, Pennsylvania.

Iverson, Brig. Gen. Alfred. *Reports of Iverson, C. S. Army, commanding brigade. June 3-August 1, 1863. — The Gettysburg Campaign.* Official Record.

The Kiehl Murder Trial! The Trial of John Kiehl, for the Poisoning of His Wife Sarah E. Kiehl, On the 7th Day of May 1871. *Carlisle, Pennsylvania: Herald Office, 1871. A book about the trial.*

Lancaster Intelligencer, newspaper, Lancaster, Lancaster County, Pennsylvania.

Lancaster Mennonite Historical Society. Lancaster, Lancaster County, Pennsylvania. www.lmhs.org

Landis, Ira D. "The Earliest Doner Family in America," *Mennonite Research Journal,* Lancaster Mennonite Historical Society, Lancaster, Pennsylvania.

Lowe, Mark Anthony, *Patronymica Britannica, A Dictionary of Family Names of the United Kingdom.* London: John Russel Smith, 1860.

Massachusetts State Archive: Massachusetts Soldiers and Sailors of the Revolutionary War.

McThomson, Lieutenant Colonel James. "Numbers 50. Report of Lieutenant Colonel James McThomson, 107th Pennsylvania Infantry." gettysburg.stonesentinels.com/union-monuments/pennsylvania/pennsylvania-infantry/107th-pennsylvania/official-report-for-the-107th-pennsylvania/

Mills, Curt. "U.S. Still Paying a Civil War Pension," *U.S. News & World Report.* 8 August 2016, www.usnews.com/news/articles/2016-08-08/civil-war-vets-pension-still-remains-on-governments-payroll-151-years-after-last-shot-fired

Mintzer, Dr. St. John Mintzer, "A surgeon on the Peninsula: Dr. St. John Watkins Mintzer's report to the Surgeon General, 30 June 1862." *US National Library of Medicine*, National Institutes of Health. www.ncbi.nlm.nih.gov/pubmed/9433116

National Archives and Records Administration (NARA):

"1790 United States Census," Franklin County, Pennsylvania.

"1800 Pennsylvania Septennial Census," Hamiltonban Township, Adams County, Pennsylvania.

"1800 United States Census, Hamiltonban Township, Adams County, Pennsylvania.

"1810 United States Census," Hamiltonban Township, Adams County, Pennsylvania.

"1810 United State Census," Menallen Township, Adams County, Pennsylvania.

"1820 United States Census," Delmar Township, Tioga County, Pennsylvania.

"1820 United States Census," Liberty Township, Adams County, Pennsylvania.

"1830 United States Census," Liberty Township, Adams County, Pennsylvania.

"1840 United States Census," Freedom Township, Adams County, Pennsylvania.

"1840 United States Census," Girard Township, Branch County, Michigan.

"1840 United States Census," Hector Township, Potter County, Pennsylvania.

"1840 United States Census," Hamiltonban Township, Potter County, Pennsylvania.

"1840 United States Census," Liberty Township, Adams County, Pennsylvania.

"1850 United States Census," Girard Township, Branch County, Michigan.

"1850 United States Census," Hamiltonban Township, Potter County, Pennsylvania.

"1850 United States Census," Liberty Township, Adams County, Pennsylvania.

"1850 United States Census," Westfield Township, Tioga County, Pennsylvania.

"1860 United States Census," Hamiltonban Township, Adams County, Pennsylvania.

"1860 United States Census," Hector Township, Potter County, Pennsylvania.

"1860 United States Census," Metal Township, Franklin County, Pennsylvania.

"1870 United States Census," Deerfield Township, Mecosta County, Michigan.

"1870 United States Census," Douglass Township, Montcalm County, Michigan.

"1870 United States Census," Guilford Township, Franklin County, Pennsylvania.

"1870 United States Census," Hamiltonban Township, Adams County, Pennsylvania.

"1880 United States Census," Chambersburg, Franklin County, Pennsylvania.

"1880 United States Census," Dickinson Township, Cumberland County, Pennsylvania.

"1880 United States Census," Douglass Township, Montcalm County, Michigan.

"1880 United States Census," Hamiltonban Township, Adams County, Pennsylvania.

"1890 US Special Census Schedule. — Surviving Soldiers, Sailors, and Marines, and Widows, etc." Various locations as cited.

"1900 United States Census," Hamiltonban Township, Adams County, Pennsylvania.

"1910 United States Census," Fairfield, Adams County, Pennsylvania.

National Tribune, newspaper, Washington, District of Columbia.

New Oxford Item, newspaper, New Oxford, Adams County, Pennsylvania.

New York Times, newspaper, New York, New York.

PA-Roots, Inc. www.pa-roots.com

"Panic of 1893," *Ohio History Connection.* www.ohiohistorycentral.org/w/Panic_of_1893

"Panic of 1893," en.wikipedia.org/wiki/Panic_of_1893Pennsylvania Historical and Museum Commission. www.phmc.pa.gov/Archives/Research-Online/Pages/Civil-War.aspx

Pennsylvania State Archives, *Pennsylvania Museum Commission*, Harrisburg, Pennsylvania.

People's Register, newspaper, Chambersburg, Franklin County, Pennsylvania.

Petruzzi, J. David and Stanley, Steven. "They Came with Barbarian Yells and Smoking Pistols" *American Battlefield Trust*, www.battlefields.org/learn/articles/they-came-barbarian-yells-and-smoking-pistols

Philadelphia Times, newspaper, Philadelphia, Pennsylvania.

Prechtel-Kluskens, Claire. "A Reasonable Degree of Promptitude, Civil War Pension Application Processing, 1861-1885." *Prologue* (Spring 2010, Volume 42, Number 1).

Proceedings of the 37th Annual Encampment of the Department of Pennsylvania Grand Army of the Republic at Allentown, June 3d and 4th, 1903. Harrisburg, Pennsylvania: Wm. Stanley Ray, State Printer of Pennsylvania, 1908.

Public Opinion, newspaper, Chambersburg, Franklin County, Pennsylvania.

Randall, George L. *DeMaranville Genealogy, Descendants of Louis DeMaranville*. New Bedford, Massachusetts, 1921.

The Record, newspaper, Hackensack, New Jersey.

Reading Times, newspaper, Reading, Berks County, Pennsylvania.

Reily, John Timon, *Conewago, A Collection of Catholic Local History Gathered From the Field of Catholic Missionary Labor Within Our Reach*. Martinsburg, West Virginia: Herald Printing, 1885.

Reynolds, John F., Major-General of Volunteers, Commanding; May 1863; Itinerary of the Corps, April 19-May 26. April 27-May 6, 1863.— *The Chancellorsville Campaign*. Official Record. civilwarhome.com/reynoldschancellorsvilleor.html

Ridgeway, Harry. *Civil War Relicman*. www.relicman.com

Roath, Capt. Emanuel D. "Numbers 51. Report of Captain Emanuel D. Roath, 107th Pennsylvania Infantry." gettysburg.stonesentinels.com/union-monuments/pennsylvania/pennsylvania-infantry/107th-pennsylvania/official-report-for-the-107th-pennsylvania/

Robinson, George Franklin Robinson, *Letter*. Company A, 7th South Carolina Infantry Regiment, Kershaw's Brigade, 18 July 1863.

Robson, Charles. *Manufactories & Manufacturers of Pennsylvania of the Nineteenth Century*. Galaxy Publishing Company, 1875, cited at "Willliam H. Horstmann & Sons, Manufacturers of Dress Trimmings and Military Goods. 5th & Cherry Streets, Philadelphia, PA." www.workshopoftheworld.com/center_city/horstmann.html

Ronig, Walter. *Michigan Place Names. Grosse Pointe, Michigan: 1973*. Republished by Great Lakes Books, Waynes University Press, Detroit, 1986.

Rose, Albert Louis, *York, York County, Pennsylvania: notebook. "Sanders Gen. General Info & sources of Peter Sanders Family. Pennsylvania church records of Saint Mary's Catholic, Fairfield, Adams County, Saint Rita Catholic, Blue Ridge Summit, Franklin County; Saint Johns Lutheran Church, Fairfield, Adams County, Saint Josephs Cemetery, Emmitsburg, Frederick County, Maryland, The Pines Church, New Chester, Pennsylvania, Saint Francis Xavier Catholic Cemetery, Gettysburg, Adams County, Pennsylvania."* York, Pennsylvania, circa 1994.

Sandberg, Carl. *Abraham Lincoln, The War Years*. New York: Harcourt Brace and Company, 1939.

The Sentinel, newspaper, Carlisle, Cumberland County, Pennsylvania.

Shannon, Fred Albert *The Organization and Administration of the Union Army, 1861-1865*. Cleveland, Ohio: The Arthur H. Clark Company, 1928.

Schenck, John S. *The History of Ionia & Montcalm Counties, Michigan*. Philadelphia: D. W. Ensign & Co., 1881.

Shippensburg News, newspaper, Shippensburg, Cumberland County, Pennsylvania.

Smith, James M. *Letter*. 25 July 1863, Company G, 149th New York Infantry. New York State Library.

"Springfield Model 1861," www.civilwaracademy.com/springfield-model-1861

Stanton Weekly Clipper, newspaper, Stanton, Montcalm County, Michigan.

Thillmann, John H., *Civil War Cavalry & Artillery Sabers*, Andrew Mowbray Publishers, 2001.

Thomas, Mary Warner and Sauers, Richard A., editors. *The Civil War Letters of First Lieutenant James B. Thomas*. Baltimore: Butternut and Blue, 1995.

Thomas, Sarah Sites; Smith, Tim; Kross, Gary; Thomas, Dean S. *Fairfield in the Civil War*. Gettysburg, Pennsylvania: Thomas Publications; Fairfield Sesquicentennial Committee. 2011.

Thompson, Richard. "Galeton Hit 4213 Population in 1904." Potter County Historical Society. *Historical Sketches of Potter County, Pennsylvania*. Coudersport, Pennsylvania: Journal Press, 1976.

Trowbridge, General L.[uther] S.[tephen]. *A Brief History of the Tenth Michigan Cavalry*. Detroit: Frieseman Bros. Printing Co., 1908.

United States Congressional Serial Set, 61st Congress, 3d Session, December 5, 1910 - March 4, 1911. Senate Reports, Washington: Government Printing office, 1911.

Valley Spirit, newspaper, Chambersburg, Franklin County, Pennsylvania.

Valley Times-Star, newspaper, Newville, Cumberland County, Pennsylvania.

Waite, Edward F. "Veteran's Pensions: The Law and Its Administration From the Revolutionary War to the Civil War," *Harper's.* Text from: Library of Congress American Memory Collection, socialwelfare.library.vcu.edu/social-security/veterans-pensions-early-history/

York Dispatch, newspaper, York, York County, Pennsylvania.

York Gazette, newspaper, York, York County, Pennsylvania.

§§§

Other books by the author:

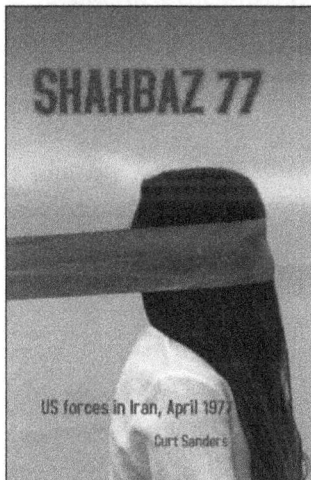

Details:
- **ISBN-13**: 9781732453807
- **ISBN-10**: 1732453802
- **Publisher**: Curt Sanders
- **Publish Date**: June 2018
- **Page Count**: 94
- **Dimensions**: 9 x 6 x 0.23 inches
- **Shipping Weight**: 0.33 pounds

Available at:
- **Amazon.com**
- **BarnesAndNoble.com**
- **BookAMillion.com**
- **iBook app**
- **indiebound.com**
- **Lulu.com**

SHAHBAZ 77
by Curt Sanders

Overview - In April 1977, the Central Treaty Organization (CENTO) with the United States Air Forces in Europe (USAFE) launched a small, but significant exercise to Shiraz, Iran. What was its purpose other than "training"? Events later show it was a first in rapid deployment models, and a match that ignited the first fire of major US tumult in the Middle East. This is a first person true story.

Paperback $7.77
This item is Non-Returnable.

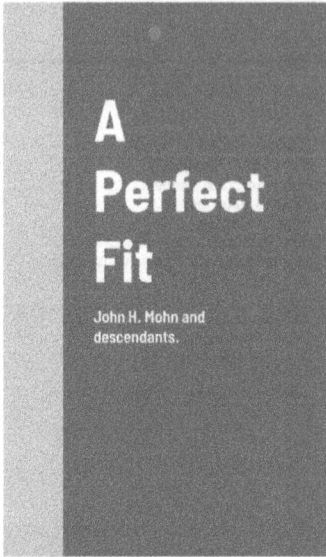

A Perfect Fit

John H. Mohn and descendants.

Details:
- **ISBN:** 9 781105 527630
- **Publisher:** Curt Sanders
- **Publish Date:** July 2021
- **Page Count:** 166
- **Dimensions:** 9 x 6 x 0.375 inches
- **Shipping Weight:** 0.625 pounds

Available At:
- **Lulu.com**

A PERFECT FIT
John H. Mohn and descendants.
by Curt Sanders

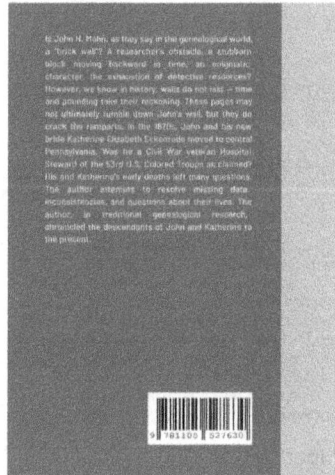

Paperback $9.99
This item is Non-Returnable

About the author

The trek into family genealogy and history grabbed Curt Sanders early in life but solidified around age sixteen. After drinking-in anecdotal stories of his great-grandmother's kin pioneering in Michigan and other places, the thirst was insatiable. He wanted to know more. The beginnings were amateurish, *ad hoc*, and with the usual interfering stop-n-start ebbs of life situations and duties.

While never forgetting his origins, it was not until his posting as a member of the U.S. Air Force to the United Kingdom in 1975-1977 that interest was re-kindled. It was also 1976: Alex Haley published *Roots: The Saga of an American Family* and the bi-centennial of the United States. Curt was living in the Fenlands of the mother country, poking around the churches and cemeteries. The "locals" would often ask: "do you have roots in the U.K.?" He could give some answers, but not enough.

Upon military discharge in 1980, he attended college. The curriculums gave him the skills to research and write the copious papers required by demanding professors.

Curt worked in the publishing industry but also spent twenty years with the Commonwealth of Pennsylvania, retiring 2015 as a data management analyst. The career further honed his data sifting, collection, fact-finding, and data analysis by monitoring and maintaining the Commonwealth's databases.

Today, Curt balances his busy retired life with writing and researching at his pleasure.

ACADEMIA:
- Harrisburg Area Community College, Associate of Liberal Arts.
- Pennsylvania State University, Bachelor of Social Science.
- Boston University, Principles of Genealogy.
- New England Historic and Genealogical Society, History for Genealogists.

MEMBER OF:
- Adams County [Pennsylvania] Historical Society.
- New England Historic Genealogical Society.
- Genealogy Society of Pennsylvania.
- Franklin County [Pennsylvania] Historical Society.
- South Central Pennsylvania Genealogical Society.

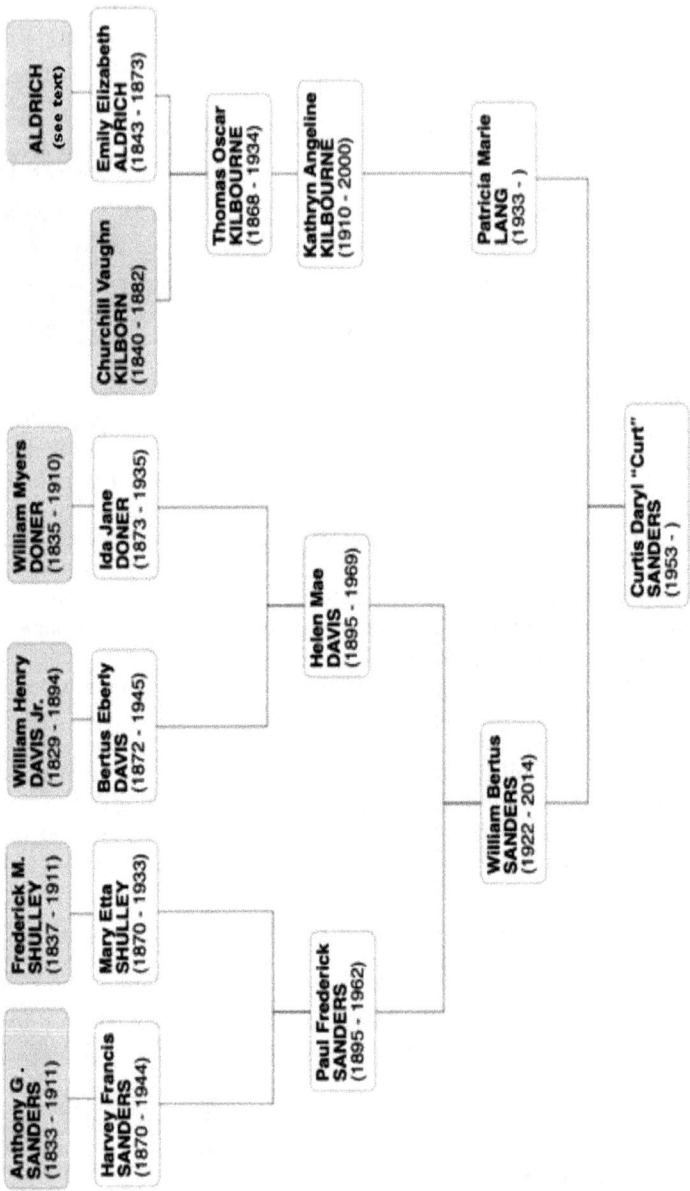

The author's pedigree tree.

www.ingramcontent.com/pod-product-compliance
Lightning Source LLC
Chambersburg PA
CBHW060018050426
42448CB00012B/2805